PYTHON PROGRAMMING

A beginners' guide to understand machine learning and master coding. Includes Smalltalk, Java, TCL, JavaScript, Perl, Scheme, Common Lisp, Data Science Analysis, C++, PHP & Ruby

By: Adam Bash

Table of Content

INTRODUCTION

The world is at a state of constant evolution towards more complexity with each passing day. Now, there are machines for almost anything. There are machines that cook, clean, and aid living even. Years ago, this would have been seen as nothing but sorcery. But is it? Of course, not. Whatever machine you can think of, be it ones as complex as factory robots or ones as simple as personal computers, each requires some programming to function. This program acts as the brain which directs the system according to the rules of its programming. So, like a matrix, this program is all around us; in our phones, homes, offices, school, you name it. This program, however, comes in different forms. But for this book, we are focusing on Python, one of the most advanced forms of programming languages.

But why Python? Why not any other language? Well, it's an easy guess. Python is arguably the most straightforward programming language to learn what with its close association with the English language in its scripting. So, unlike most other languages which are quite complicated for the average non-programmer, one can understand a few things about Python by merely picking up a book. This ease of readability is no mistake in any sense. As a matter of fact, it is in its very design. Tons of multinational companies like Google, even NASA, use Python in their programming because it is easier to maintain and reuse. Python has only come this far as a programming language because of its features which are integral to the future. It is why everyone must have a basic knowledge of it.

So, come along on this fun adventure of learning Python, as we take you through the basics of the language. Learn, experiment, and have fun!

CHAPTER 1: HISTORY OF PYTHON

Python as a programming language took off in the later periods of the 1980s by Guido van Rossum, but no implementation was made until December of 1989. At the time, Van Rossum worked at Centrum Voor Wiskunde en Informatica (CWI) in the Netherlands where he was employed to implement a programming language known as ABC. Van Rossum's contract to work on the AMOEBA project heralded the birth of Python as a programming language of its own due to certain flaws on the part of the former. The features of ABC were the major influencing points which pushed Van Rossum into designing and developing Python, as a means of overcoming the inhibitions the former posed.

These inhibitions rose when Van Rossum began working on a project, name of AMOEBA during the period before Python's conception. AMOEBA was a new distributed operating system which was required to be coded with a scripting language having syntax. The only programming language with such qualities was ABC, but its inability to access the system calls in AMOEBA became its undoing.

Thus, Van Rossum sought a way to overcome this flaw in the ABC programming language. He tried seeking out scripting languages with similar syntax builds to ABC, but different in the ability to have access to AMOEBA system calls. His efforts to find a suitable scripting language with such features proved futile. So, to make up for this absence in an appropriate scripting language; Van Rossum began the creation of a new scripting language. One which would prove helpful in overcoming the flaws posed by the ABC. Van Rossum started work on the new programming language well into the late periods of 1980 and went on to introduce the first version of the Python programming language in 1991. This first release which came with the features of a module system obtained from Modula-3; was codenamed Python by Van Rossum.

Why "Python"?

Of all the things that he could name his programming language after, why did Van Rossum pick the name "python"? Did he have a pet python he was especially fond of, or is the name an acronym for a much meaningful whole? Neither. Even though the logo of the scripting language is designed with two snakes in the picture, the conceptualization of the name cannot be traced to any known snake.

Guido van Rossum's choice of the name "Python" can instead be traced back to English humor. In his 1996 writings, Van Rossum stated that he so named the programming language when he was in an unserious mood, and for his love of a comedy show aired on the BBC, Monty Python Flying Circus.

The Role of Van Rossum in the development of Python

until the date Being the principal author and designer of the programming language, Guido Van Rossum played a crucial role in the development of the programming language across different versions and years. His continued contribution to the evolution and promotion of Python, saw him bestowed upon the title of BDFL, an acronym for Benevolent Dictator for Life by the Python community. However, in 2018, the 12th of July precisely, Van Rossum made an announcement of his retirement from the title of BDFL. Before that, Van Rossum made a funding proposal to DARPA in 1999, name of, Computer Programming for Everybody. It was in this proposal Van Rossum outlined his aims for the development of Python as a programming language. Some of those goals are;

- To create a code which can be understood like plain English language.

- To create an easy to use and intuitive language which is just as influential as other significant contemporaries.

- To create a programming language which is suitable for use in everyday activities, allowing for quicker development durations.

- To create an open source such that anyone can get involved and contribute to developing the program.

Versions Of Python

Since Its Conception With Guido van Rossum at the helm of affairs, Python has witness three versions over the years since its conception in the '80s. These versions represent the growth, development, and evolution of the scripting language over time, and cannot be done without in telling the history of Python.

The Versions Of Python Include The Following;

- **Python 0.9.0:**

The first-ever version of Python released following its implementation and in-house releases at the Centrum Wiskunde and Informatica (CWI) between the years 1989 and 1990, was tagged version 0.9.0. This early version which was released on alt.sources had features such as exception handling, functions, and classes with inheritance, as well as the core data types of list, str, dict, among others in its development. The first release came with a module system obtained from Module-3, which Van Rossum defined as one of the central programming units used in the development of Python. Another similarity the first release bore with Module-3 is found in the exception model which comes with an added else clause. With the public release of this early version came a flurry of users which culminated in the formation of a primary discussion forum for Python in 1994.

The group was named comp.lang.python and served as a milestone for the growing popularity of Python users. Following the release of the first version in the 29th of February, 1991, there were seven other updates made to the early version 0.9.0. These updates took varying tags under the 0.9.0 version and were spread out over nearly three years (1991 to 1993). The first version update came in the form of

Python 0.9.1, which was released in the same month of February 1991 as its predecessor. The next update came in the autumn period of the release year, under the label Python 0.9.2. By Christmas Eve of the same year (1991) python published its third update to the earliest version under the label Python 0.9.4. By January of the succeeding year, the 2nd precisely, a gift update under the label Python 0.9.5 was released. By the 6th of April, 1992, a sixth update followed named, Python 0.9.6.

It wasn't until the next year, 1993, that a seventh update was released under the tag Python 0.9.8. The eighth and final update to the earliest version came five months after the seventh, on the 29th of July, 1993, and was dubbed python 0.9.9. These updates marked the first generation of python development before it transcended into the next version label.

• **Python 1.0**

After the last update to Python 0.9.0, a new version, Python 1.0, was released in January of the following year. 1994 marked the addition of key new features to the Python programming language. Functional programming tools such as map, reduce, filter, and lambda were part of the new features of the version 1 release. Van Rossum mentioned that the obtainment of map, lambda, reduce and filter was made possible by a LISP hacker who missed them and submitted patches that worked. Van Rossum's contract with CWI came to an end with the release of the first update version 1.2 on the 10th of April, 1995. In the same year, Van Rossum went on to join CNRI (Corporation for National Research Initiatives) in Reston, Virginia, United States, where he continued to work on Python and published different version updates. Nearly six months following the first version update, version 1.3 was released on the 12th of October, 1995. The third update, version 1.4, came almost a year later in October of 1996.

By then, Python had developed numerous added features. Some of the typical new features included an inbuilt support system for complex numbers and keyword arguments which, although inspired by Modula-3, shared a bit of a likeness to the keyword arguments of Common Lisp. Another included feature was a simple form hiding data through name mangling, although it could be easily bypassed. It was during his days at CNRI that Van Rossum began the CP4E (Computer Programming for Everybody) program which was aimed at making more people get easy access to programming by engaging in simple literacy of programming languages. Python was a pivotal element to van Rossum's campaign, and owing to its concentration on clean forms of syntax; Python was an already suitable programming language. Also, since the goals of ABC and CP4E were quite similar, there was no hassle putting Python to use.

The program was pitched to and funded by DARPA, although it did become inactive in 2007 after running for eight years. However, Python still tries to be relatively easy to learn by not being too arcane in its semantics and syntax, although no priority is made of reaching out to non-programmers again.

The year 2000 marked another significant step in the development of Python when the python core development team switched to a new platform — BeOpen.com where a new group, BeOpen PythonLabs team was formed. At the request of CNRI, a new version update 1.6 was released on the 5th of September, succeeding the fourth version update (Python 1.5) on the December of 1997. This update marked the complete cycle of development for the programming language at CNRI because the development team left shortly afterward. This change affected the timelines of release for the new version Python 2.0 and the version 1.6 update; causing them to clash. It was only a question of time before Van Rossum, and his crew of PythonLabs developers switched to Digital Creations, with Python 2.0 as the only version ever released by BeOpen.com.

With the version 1.6 release caught between a switch of platforms, it didn't take long for CNRI to include a license in the version release of Python 1.6. The license contained in the release was quite more prolonged than the previously used CWI license, and it featured a clause mentioning that the license was under the protection of the laws applicable to the State of Virginia. This intervention sparked a legal feud which led The Free Software Foundation into a debate regarding the "choice-of-law" clause being incongruous with that if the GNU General Public License. At this point, there was a call to negotiations between FSF, CNRI, and BeOoen regarding changing to Python's free software license which would serve to make it compatible with GPL. The negotiation process resulted in the release of another version update under the name of Python 1.6.1. This new version was no different from its predecessor in any way asides a few new bug fixes and the newly added GPL-compatible license.

- **Python 2.0:**

After the many legal dramas surrounding the release of the second-generation Python 1.0 which corroborated into the release of an unplanned update (version 1.6.1), Python was keen to put all behind and forge ahead. So, in October of 2000, Python 2.0 was released. The new release featured new additions such as list comprehensions which were obtained from other functional programming languages Haskell and SETL. The syntax of this latest version was akin to that found in Haskell, but different in that Haskell used punctuation characters while Python stuck to alphabetic keywords. Python 2.0 also featured a garbage collection system which was able to collect close reference cycles. A version update (Python 2.1) quickly followed the release of Python 2.0, as did Python 1.6.1. However, due to the legal issue over licensing, Python renamed the license on the new release to Python Software Foundation License.

As such, every new specification, code or documentation added from the release of version update 2.1 was owned and protected by the PSF (Python Software Foundation) which was a nonprofit organization created in the year 2001. The organization was designed similarly to the Apache Software Foundation. The release of version 2.1 came with changes made to the language specifications, allowing support of nested scopes such as other statically scoped languages. However, this feature was, by default, not in use and unrequired until the release of the next update, version 2.2 on the 21st of December, 2001.

Python 2.2 came with a significant innovation of its own in the form of a unification of all Python's types and classes. The unification process merged the types coded in C and the classes coded in Python into a single hierarchy. The unification process caused Python's object model to remain totally and continuously object-oriented. Another significant innovation was the addition of generators as inspired by Icon. Two years after the release of version 2.2, version 2.3 was published in July of 2003. It was nearly another two years before version 2.4 was released on the 30th of November in 2004. Version 2.5 came less than a year after Python 2.4, in September of 2006. This version introduced a "with" statement containing a code block in a context manager; as in obtaining a lock before running the code block and releasing the lock after that or opening and closing a file. The block of code made for behavior similar to RAII (Resource Acquisition Is Initialization) and swapped the typical "try" or "finally" idiom. The release of version 2.6 on the 1st of

October, 2008 was strategically scheduled such that it coincided with the release of Python 3.0.

Asides the proximity in release date, version 2.6 also had some new features like the "warnings" mode which outlined the use of elements which had been omitted from Python 3.0. Subsequently, in July of 2010, another update to Python 2.0 was released in the version of python 2.7. The new version updates shared features and coincided in release with version 3.1 — the first version update of python 3. At this time, Python drew an end to the release of Parallel 2.x and 3.x, making python 2.7 the last version update of the 2.x series. Python went public in 2014, November precisely, to announce to its username that the availability of python 2.7 would stretch until 2020. However, users were advised to switch to python 3 in their earliest convenience.

• **Python 3.0:**

The fourth generation of Python, Python 3.0, otherwise known as Py3K and python 3000, was published on the 3rd of December 2008. This version was designed to fix the fundamental flaws in the design system of the scripting language. A new version number had to be made to implement the required changes which could not be run while keeping the stock compatibility of the 2.x series that was by this time redundant. The guiding rule for the creation of python 3 was to limit the duplication of features by taking out old formats of processing stuff. Otherwise, Python three still followed the philosophy with which the previous versions were made. Albeit, as Python had evolved to accumulate new but redundant ways of programming alike tasks, python 3.0 was emphatically targeted at quelling duplicative modules and constructs in keeping with the philosophy of making one "and preferably only one" apparent way of doing things. Regardless of these changes, though, version 3.0 maintained a multi-paradigm language, even though it didn't share compatibility with its predecessor.

The lack of compatibility meant Python 2.0 codes were unable to be run on python 3.0 without proper modifications. The dynamic typing used in Python as well as the intention to change the semantics of specific methods of dictionaries, for instance, made a perfect mechanical conversion from the 2.x series to version 3.0 very challenging. A tool, name of 2to3, was created to handle the parts of translation which could be automatically done. It carried out its tasks quite successfully, even though an early review stated that the tool was incapable of handling certain aspects of the conversion process. Proceeding the release of version 3.0, projects that required compatible with both the 2.x and 3.x series were advised to be given a singular base for the 2.x series.

The 3.x series platform, on the other hand, was to produce releases via the 2to3 tool. For a long time, editing the Python 3.0 codes were forbidden because they required being run on the 2.x series. However, now, it is no longer necessary. The reason being that in 2012, the recommended method was to create a single code base which could run under the 2.x and 3.x series through compatibility modules. Between the December of 2008 and July 2019, 8 version updates have been published under the python 3.x series. The current version as at the 8th of July 2019 is the Python 3.7.4. Within this timeframe, many updates have been made to the programming language, involving the addition of new features mentioned below:

1. Print which used to be a statement was changed to an inbuilt function, making it relatively easier to swap out a module in utilizing different print functions as well as regularizing the syntax. In the late versions of the 2.x series, (python 2.6 and 2.7), print is introduced as inbuilt, but is concealed by a syntax of the print

statement which is capable of being disabled by entering the following line of code into the top of the file: from__future__import print_function

2. The [input] function in the Python 2.x series was removed, and the [raw_input] function to [input] was renamed. The change was such that the [input] function of Python 3 behaves similarly to the [raw_input] function of the python 2.x series; meaning input is typically outputted in the form of strings instead of being evaluated as a single expression.

3. [reduce] was removed with the exemption of [map] and [filter] from the in-built namespace into [functools]. The reason behind this change is that operations involving [reduce] are better expressed with the use of an accumulation loop.

4. Added support was provided for optional function annotations which could be used in informal type declarations as well as other purposes.

5. The [str]/[unicode] types were unified, texts represented, and immutable bytes type were introduced separately as well as a mutable [bytearray]

type which was mostly corresponding; both of which indicate several arrays of bytes.

6. Taking out the backward-compatibility features such as implicit relative imports, old-style classes, and string exceptions.

7. Changing the mode of integer division functionality. For instance, in the Python 2.x series, 5/2 equals 2. Note that in the 3.x series, 5/2 equals 2.5. From the recent versions of the 2.x series beginning from version 2.2 up until python 3: 5//2 equals 2.

In contemporary times, version releases in the version 3.x series have all been equipped with added, substantial new features; and every ongoing development on Python is being done in line with the 3.x series.

CHAPTER 2: BASIC CONCEPTS OF PYTHON PROGRAMMING

In python programming, the English language is mainly used in coding many keywords. The mastery of these keywords means knowledge of the fundamental aspects of python programming. However, before delving into these primary keywords, you have to understand the basic concepts associated with Python. These concepts are necessary to understand every other aspect of the scripting language. Below, a detailed outline is given in these basic concepts.

Properties:

Python is typically typed in an implicit and dynamic format; hence, there is no requirement to declare variables. These types are enforced, and the variables are sensitive to cases. For instance, bar and VAR are considered to be two distinct variables in themselves. There is no definite array of characters used to terminate statements in Python.

The use of indentations specifies blocks; thus, to begin a block you indent, and to end it, you de-dent. Any statement which expects a level of indentation is concluded using a colon sign. The sign (#) is used in each line to add comments. In making multi-line comments, multi-line strings have to be used.

Assigning values is done using the sign (=) and equality testing are carried out with the use of two signs of equality (==). Values can be incremented or decremented with the value on the right side using the operators (+=) and (-=). Operations of this sort can also be done on strings as well as other data types. Multiple variables can also be used on a single line.

Variables:

Consider variables to be a word which codes, stores, or contains a value. In python programming, defining a variable and assigning a value to it is a relatively straightforward process. For instance, if you want to store a number, you can assign it to a variable. You could assign 5 to a variable named "five." You can assign a value to any variable of your choice.

The variable "two" stores the integer 2, and "some_number" is used to store 10000. Asides integers, booleans (True or

False), float, strings, among others constitute the data types used in python programming.

• Looping and Iterator:

There are several forms of iteration in python programming, but in this segment, only two would be talked about. — "for" and "while."

• While Looping:

While the statement entered is True, the code passed into the block would be run. The code would proceed to print numbers 1 to 10. A loop condition is needed to run a while loop, and should it continue being True, iteration continues. Let's consider an example of a variable "num." When NUM is 11, the loop condition evaluates to False. That is, iteration would continue until it is set to False.

• For Looping:

When a variable "num" is passed to the block, the "for" statement iterates it. The code would print similarly as the "while" code from numbers 1 to 10.

• Quotation:

String literals are denoted by single ('), double (") or triple ("''
or """) quotes in Python, provided the type of quote used to begin the string is used to end it as well. In spanning the string across multiple lines, the three quotes (''' or """) is usually used. Let's consider an example below;

word = 'word'

sentence = "This is a sentence."

paragraph = """This is a paragraph.

It is made up of multiple lines and sentences."""

• Python Identifiers:

A python identifier refers to a name used in showing the identity of a function, variable, class, object, or module. Identifies typically begin with a letter from a to z, or A to Z or an underscore (_) closely succeeded by zero or more underscores, digits (0 to 9) and letters. In Python, punctuation characters like modulus (%), at (@) and the dollar sign ($) are not allowed as identifiers. Moreover, as was earlier discussed, Python is case sensitive and would interpret Manpower and manpower as two distinct identifiers in themselves. Below are some naming conditions for Python identifiers: All class names begin with a first letter in the uppercase while other identifiers begin with lower case letters. Beginning an identifier with one leading underscore is an indication of a private identifier. On the other hand, starting with two leading underscores shows that the identifier is strongly private. Should the identifier end with two trailing underscores, the identifier is said to be a language-defined special name.

• **Suites:**

Suites refer to a group of individual statements which combine to form a single block of code. Complex statements like while, if, class and def need a suite and a header line. Header lines start a statement with a keyword and are terminated by using a colon sign (:) which is closely succeeded by one or multiple lines which constitute the construct of the suite. For instance;

if expression:

Suite

elif expression:

Suite else:

Suite

• Importing:

In python programming, external libraries can be accessed by using a specific keyword; import[library]. For individual functions, you can use [libname] or [funcname] to import. Let's consider an example below:

syntax:

import random

from time import clock

• Strings:

Strings are made using single or double quotation marks. It is also possible to use quotation marks of a specific kind in a string which uses a different one.

As such, the following string is valid in Python:

"This is a 'valid' string."

Multi-strings are contained in single, double, or triple quotation marks. Python can support Unicode from the very start when using the syntax outlined below:

"This is Unicode."

In filling strings with values, the modulo (%) operator is used alongside a tuple. Each module is swapped out for a tuple item, proceeding to the right from the left. Dictionary substitutions can also be used in such cases.

- **Functions:**

The keyword 'def' is used in the declaration of functions. By assigning default values to them, optional arguments can be placed in the function declaration behind mandatory arguments. Should named arguments arise, a value is attached to the argument name. Functions can be in a tuple, and several values can be effectively returned by using tuple unpacking. Parameters are transmitted via reference, but strings, ints, tuples, as well as other immutable types are unchangeable. The reason being that only the memory location of the item is sent. In binding another object to the variable, the older one is taken out, and immutable types are replaced.

- **Data types:**

In Python, every value is assigned a specified datatype. Since every aspect of Python consists of an object, data types are in fact classes, and variables are instances or objects of these classes. Python has several data types used in its operations. Listed below are some of the basic, important ones.

Python Numbers:

Python numbers is a category constituted by floating-point numbers and integers as well as complex numbers. They are usually defined as int (integer), float (floating number), and complex (complex numbers) class in Python.

To determine the class a value or variable belongs in the type() function is used, and to find out if an object belongs in a specific class, the isinstance() function is used. In python numbers, the length of integers is boundless and can only be limited by the amount of available memory.

Also, a floating-point number can maintain accuracy up to 15 decimal places. The presence of a decimal point shows the distinction between an integer and floating points. For example, 1 and 1.0 are the same in basic maths, but in Python, the former (1) is an integer, and the latter (1.0) is a floating number.

Complex numbers are usually written in the following format, x + y; where x constitutes the real part of the equation, and the imaginary part is denoted by y.

Python List:

A list refers to an ordered sequence of items. In python programming, list is one of the widely used datatypes owing to its relative flexibility. The items contained in a list do not have to share similarities in type to be on the list. Also, the process of declaring a list is quite easy. Items which are separated using commas and are contained within brackets []. The slicing operator [] is used in extracting a specific range of items or a single item from a list. In Python, index begins from the number 0. Lists can be mutable, meaning the value of the elements in a list is capable of being changed.

Python Tuple:

In Python, a tuple refers to an ordered sequence of items similar to list. The distinction, however, is that unlike lists, tuples are immutable. That is, once they have been created, the elements of a tuple cannot be changed or modified. Tuples are mainly used in place of lists to write-protect data as they are much faster and are incapable of changing dynamically. Tuples are defined with parentheses () where the items within are separated using commas. Moreover, even though a slicing operator [] can also be used to extract items, the values cannot be changed.

Python Set:

A set is a collection of special items which are not in any particular order. It is defined by values contained within braces {} and separated using commas. Like sets in basic mathematics, operations can be carried out on python sets such as the intersection and union of two sets. Every set has a unique value, and since they are unordered, they do not require indexing. In this vein, the slicing operator [] cannot be used on sets.

Python Dictionary:

Like sets, python dictionary is a collection of key-value pairs in an unordered state. Dictionaries are used when there are vast volumes of data. Dictionaries are optimized to retrieve data. To do this, the key to retrieve a specific value must be known. In python programming, dictionaries exist as items being paired in the format key:value and contained within braces {}.

Moreover, the pair must not necessarily be of the same type. That is, key and value can be different types. In the pair, the key is used to retrieve a respective value, but it doesn't work vice versa.

Conversion between data types:

Conversion can be done from one data type to another using a several type conversion functions such as str(), float(), int() among others. In converting from float to int, the value would be truncated to make it nearer to zero. Only compatible values can be used in converting from and to string. Conversion can also be done from one sequence to another sequence. In converting to dictionary, every element must exist as a pair.

What are iterators in Python?

Iterators exist in every aspect of python programming. They can be found implemented in generators, comprehensions, for loops, and so on, but they are hidden away from plain sight. An iterator is merely an object which can be iterated upon. That is, an iterator refers to any object which returns data at the rate of one element per time.

Python iterator objects have to implement two special methods, namely, __iter__() and __next__(). Collectively, both special methods are known as the iterator protocol. An object is only iterable if an iterator can be obtained from it.

Many of the in-built containers in python programming, such as string, tuple, list, etcetera are iterables. The items of an iterator can be iterated through manually using a next() function. If at the end of an iteration process, there isn't any more data that can be iterated, the function would raise a StopIteration.

Infinite Iterators:

The items in an iterator object must not necessarily be exhausted. Infinite iterators exist, and they never end. Such iterators require thorough caution to handle.

It isn't compulsory to use up all the items in an iterator object.

There can be Infinite iterators (which never ends). We must be careful when handling such iterator.

Type Conversion:

Type conversion refers to a process of converting the value of a specific data type (string, integer, etcetera) to another data type. In python programming, there are two types of type conversion, namely:

1. Implicit Type Conversion

2. Explicit Type Conversion Implicit

Type Conversion:

Implicit type conversions are automatically done by Python in a process in which the system converts one data type to a different type. Since Python handles the conversion, no external involvement by a user is required. An example of implicit type conversion can be seen in the conversion of a lower data type to a higher data type, as in integer to float.

Explicit Type Conversion:

Explicit type conversion requires a user to convert the data type of an object to another data type needed of them. Predefined functions such as float(), str(), int(), among others are used in the process of explicit type conversion.

This type conversion can also be known as typecasting; the reason being that the user is required to cast (change) the data type of the objects. Typecasting is done by assigning a needed data type function to an expression. An example of explicit type conversion can be seen in the addition of string and integer.

• Python Variables:

In Python, a variable refers to any named location used in the storing of data to memory. Variables can be seen as containers which hold data that can be modified over time throughout the programming process. For instance, number = 10. In this instance, a named variable (number) is created, and the value (10) has been assigned to it. Consider variables similar to a box used to store clothes. Moreover, those clothes are capable of being replaced at any point in time. Keep in mind that in python programming, values can't be assigned to variables, in as much as Python provides reference of the object (value) to the variable. As is evident in the example, the assignment operator (=) is used to assign values to variables.

• Constants:

Constants refer to any type of variable whose value is incapable of being changed. Consider constants to be containers which hold information that cannot be replaced over time, or a box containing clothes, which once stored, cannot again be taken out and replaced. Constants have to be declared and assigned on a module in Python. Here, the module signifies a new file filled with functions, variables, and so on which are imported to the main file. In a module, constants have all their characters written in uppercases, and words are separated using underscores.

There are specific rules and naming conventions that apply for variables and constants. They are outlined below:

1. Only create sensible names. For instance, vowel is a more sensible name than v.

2. In declaring a variable, camelCase notation should be used. That is, it should begin with a lower-case letter. Take an example; myName.

3. When necessary, capital letters should be used to declare constants — for instance, PI, G, TEMP, etcetera.

4. Avoid the use of special characters such as #, %, !, $, @, among others.

5. Never begin a name using a digit.

6. Constants are to be imputed in python modules and are to remain unchanged.

7. The names of variables and constants should be a combination of letters in lowercase (a to z), uppercase (A to Z), digits (0 to 9), or underscores (_) — for

instance, limbo_case, CapWords, MACRO_CASE, etcetera.

• **Literals:**

Literals refer to raw data provided in a constant or variable. There exist several literals in Python. They include the following;

• **Numeric Literals:**

Numeric literals refer to literals which are immutable or unchangeable. They can be found under three different numerical types, namely, Complex, Float, and Integer.

• **String literals:**

String literals refer to any sequence of characters contained within quotes. As was earlier mentioned, a string can be included within single, double, or triple quotes.

• **Character Literals:**

A character literal refers to a single character enclosed in single or double quotes.

- **Boolean literals:**

Boolean literals are capable of having any of these two values: True or False.

- **Special literals:**

There exists only one special literal in Python. That is, None. It is used to indicate a field which isn't created.

- **Literal Collections:**

Literal collections are of four types, namely; Tuple literals, Set literals, List literals, and Dict literals Python Operators: Operators in Python are special symbols user to carry out logical or arithmetic computations. The values operated on by an operator are known as operands.

For instance:

>>> 4+6

10

The sign (+) is the operator in this instance, and it performs the addition on the operands 4 and 6, and 10, here, indicates the output of the operation.

Types of operators:

• **Arithmetic Operators:**

+: Used to add operands.

–: To subtract operands.

*: To multiply operands.

/: To divide the left operand by the right operand. The answer is almost always a float number.

% (Modulus): The remainder of the division of the left operand by the right.

// (Floor division): Division which results in a whole number.

** (Exponent): Left operand raised to the power of the right one.

• **Comparison operators:**

These operators are used in the comparison of values. The returns are usually True or False based on the condition entered.

> (Greater than): True when left operand is greater than the right one.

< (Less than): True when the left operand is less than the right one.

== (Equal to): True when both left and right operands are equal.

!= (Not equal to): True when both operands are not equal.

>= (Greater than or equal to): True when left operand is greater than or equal to the right operand.

<= (Less than or equal to): True when left operand is less than or equal to the right.

• **Logical operators:**

Logical operators are made up of the and, not and or operators.

and: True when both the left and right operands are true.

not: True when the operand is false.

or: True when either the left or right operands is true.

• **Bitwise operators:**

This type of operators acts on operands like they were a string of binary digits. As the name suggests, bitwise operators work one bit at a time.

&: Bitwise AND.

|: Bitwise OR.

~: Bitwise NOT.

^: Bitwise XOR.

>>: Bitwise right shift.

<<: Bitwise left shift.

- **Assignment Operators:**

Assignment Operators are used in assigning values to variables. For example, b = 5 assigns the value (5) to the left operand (a). This example is a simple assignment operator. Compound assignment operators also exist in Python.

An example is b += 7.

This operator is the same as b = b + 7. Assignment operators include; =, +=, -=, *=, /=, %=, //=, **=, &=, |=, ^=, >>=, and <<=.

- **Identity operators:**

There are two identity operators in Python, namely; is and is not. These identity operators are used to find out if two variables or values share a similar location in the memory. Keep in mind that just because two variables are equal doesn't necessarily imply that they are identical. is: True when both left and right operands are identical. That is, they refer to the same object. is not: True when both left and right operands aren't identical. That is, they don't apply to the same object.

- **Membership operators:**

There are also two types of membership operators in python programming, namely, in and not. Membership operators are used in testing if a variable or value exists in a sequence (i.e., list, set, dictionary, string, and tuple). In dictionary, the only thing that can be tested for is the presence of a key, not the value.

in: True when value or variable is found in the sequence.

not in: True when value or variable isn't found in the sequence.

CHAPTER 3: WHAT IS PYTHON?

Python refers to an interpreted and scripting language, which is object-oriented. It falls under the category of high-level programming languages and exhibits dynamic semantics. Python has high-level inbuilt data structures as well as dynamic typing and binding; making it a suitable fit for Rapid Application Development. It can also be used as a glue or scripting language for joining together already existing components. Owing to its syntax, which is relatively simple and easy to learn, Python emphasizes readability, thus curbing the cost of maintaining the program. Python also supports packages and modules which foster reusing codes and modularizing the program.

How is Python Used?

Python is a programming language which can be used for many purposes. However, most important of all, Python is an interpreted language; meaning that during run-time, its written code isn't converted into a format that is readable by the computer. Whereas, many programming languages require this translation to be done before the program can be run. Programming languages with such qualities were known as scripting language in the past because they were used to carry out trivial tasks. Albeit, this nomenclature changed as a result of Python. The reason being that it is commonplace for broad applications to be written almost exclusively in Python in contemporary times.

The application of Python can be used in the following ways:

1. In working with Files

2. In programming CGI for Web Applications

3. In reading from and Writing to PostgreSQL

4. In building RSS Readers

5. In reading from and writing to MySQL

6. In creating Calendars in HTML

How Python Compares to Other Languages:

Owing to its popularity, Python is commonly brought under comparison with other interpreted languages inclusive but not limited to the following; Smalltalk, Java, TCL, JavaScript, Perl, etcetera. There are also some comparisons made to Scheme, Common Lisp and C++. In comparing Python to these languages, the focus would be placed on issues regarding each language alone. Technically, the choice of any programming language depends on other apparent factors like training, cost, prior investment, availability, and sometimes even sentiments. Hence, this section is not an advantage comparison to prove what programming language is better than another.

• **Perl:**

Perl and Python share similarities in background; both of them coming from Unix scripting which they have now outgrown. Another similarity exists in the features they both have. The only concise difference between Python and Perl is found in their philosophies. Perl places emphasis on the support of basic application-oriented tasks. For example, Perl has built-in regular expression, report generating features, and file scanning. Python, on the other hand, places more support on basic methods of programming like object-oriented programming and the design of data structure. Python further goes on to support programmers in creating codes with easy readability and maintainability by offering a notation which is elegant but not too cryptic. As a result, Python comes near Perl in this regard, but seldom ever trumps the latter in its actual application domain. Albeit,

Python possesses applicability which is well over the niche Perl operates in.

- **Common Lisp and Scheme:**

Common Lisp and Scheme both share proximity with Python as a result of the dynamics of their semantics. However, they possess a distinct method of syntax which makes any comparison somewhat of a debate. The argument is whether or not Lisp's lack of syntax is advantageous or disadvantageous. Keep in mind that Python possesses introspective capabilities which are akin to those seen in Lisp. Also, Python programs can create and execute fragments of programs on the go. In this debate, factors affecting the real world are decisive elements: Common Lisp is quite large, and the world of Scheme is a fragment of many different incompatible versions, whereas, Python's implementation is both compact, single, and free.

- **Java:**

It is a general belief that python programs run somewhat slower than programs written in Java. However, they are developed much faster than Java's. In terms of length, Python programs are usually up to 3 to 5 times shorter than their equivalents in Java. This difference is primarily because of

Python's in-built features such as dynamic typing and high-level data types. For instance, a programmer would have no hassle declaring the types of variables or arguments with Python, and the dictionary types and robust polymorphic list found in Python, for which a productive syntactic support system is built into the language, is hardly ever out of use in any python program.

As a result of the run-time typing, Java's run time works significantly less hard than Python's. For instance, in the evaluation of the expression x+y, Python has first to observe both objects (x and y) to decipher their type, which at compile time is yet unknown. It then proceeds to invoke the proper addition operation, which could turn out as an overloaded method defined by the user. Conversely, Java is capable of performing a valid floating-point or integer addition but needs the variables x and y to be declared and would not allow the + operator to be overloaded in cases of user-defined classes. In this vein, Python seems better suited for the role of a "glue" language, while Java can be better used as a low-level implementation language. Different components can be developed in Java and joined to form python applications.

Conversely, Python can be used in prototyping components until their designs can be "hardened" in a Java implementation. To foster such a development a python implementation coded in Java is currently being developed and would allow the calling of python codes from Java and vice versa. In doing this, Python's source code would be converted to Java bytecode by use of a run-time library as support for the dynamic semantics of Python.

- **Smalltalk:**

The only arguable difference between Smalltalk and Python is that the latter has a more "mainstream" syntax that lends it an edge in programmer training. Dynamic typing and binding, and the fact that everything on Python being an object makes Python very much akin to Smalltalk. Albeit, Python differentiates built-in object types from user-defined classes and does not support inheritance from built-in types at the moment. The standard library of collection data in Smalltalk is better refined, while Python's library is equipped with more facilities focused on treating issues regarding the Internet and WWW realities like FTP, HTML, and email. Another distinction is evident in their different philosophies.

Python has a unique view of the development environment as well as the distribution of code. In cases where Smalltalk typically inserts a monolithic "system image" which involves both the user's program and the environment, Python saves both the standard modules and the user modules in separate files capable of being distributed or rearranged outside the system. A consequence of this is that a python program has several options for attaching a GUI (Graphical User Interface) because there is no in-built GUI in the system.

• JavaScript:

The "object-based" subset of Python is roughly equivalent to JavaScript. Unlike Java, Python supports a programming style which employs simple variables and functions without indulging in class definitions - a feature quite akin to JavaScript. Moreover, frankly, that is all there is to JavaScript. Python, however, supports the writing of much bigger programs and a better system of reusing codes via an actual object-oriented programming style, where inheritance and classes play vital roles.

• C++:

C++ contains most of the features discussed in Java, only with slight additions. While python codes are usually shorter than Java codes by up to 3 to 5 times, they are relatively 5 to 10 times shorter than their equivalents in C++. Evidence from anecdotes suggests that a single python programmer can complete what two C++ programmers won't finish in a year, in two months. Python serves as a glue language in the combination of components coded in C++.

- **Tcl:**

Similar to Python, Tcl can serve as a language for application extension, and an individual programming language in its own right. Albeit, Tcl usually saves its data as strings; meaning it its data structures are weak, and as a result, would process codes way slower than Python. Asides this, Tcl is lacking in features necessary for writing big programs like modular namespaces. Hence, while a common extensive application running on Tcl typically contains extensions coded in C++ or C which are particular to the application, its equivalent application in Python can be coded in pure Python. Moreover, the development of pure Python is a much more comfortable and quicker process than writing and debugging a C++ or C component.

It is a widespread belief that the only redeeming quality of Tcl lies in its Tk toolkit. Python adopted a similar interface to Tk for its traditional GUI component library. In addressing the problems of speed, Tcl 8.0 provides a bytecode compiler fitted with a ranged data type support system, mad additional namespaces. Albeit, regardless of these interventions, Tcl is still very much cumbersome a programming language.

• PHP:

PHP is gradually taking over as the official language of web development, displacing Perl in the process. Albeit, more than Perl or PHP, Python has better readability and can be quickly followed. The one disadvantage Perl has similar to PHP is the squirrely code. Also, coding programs which exceed the range of 50 to 100 lines become relatively more difficult as a result of the Perl and PHP's syntax. Conversely, Python is hardwired to be readable, down to the very fabric of the language. This readability makes it easier to extend and maintain programs written in Python. While PHP has begun to get more usage generally, it remains a programming language meant for the web regardless, designer to return web-readable information instead of handling system-level activities. This distinction is better exemplified by the fact that web servers coded in Python which understand PHP, but it is impossible to develop a web server in PHP which understands Python. In conclusion, unlike Python, PHP is not object-oriented. This characteristic has a significant implication on the scalability, readability, and ease of maintenance of both programs.

• Ruby:

Python is often brought in comparison with Ruby. Both of them are interpreted high-level programming languages. Their codes are usually implemented in ways that understanding the details is not a requirement. They are just taken care of. Both Python and Ruby have their basis in object-oriented programming. Their method of implementing objects and classes make for a more comfortable and better system of maintainability as well as code reuse. Both Python and Ruby are general-purpose languages and can be used in carrying out simple tasks like converting texts, or more complicated activities like managing major financial data structures and programming and controlling robots. The significant distinction between the two languages, however, lies in their flexibility and readability. Owing to its nature of being object-oriented, Ruby codes have no errors in being squirrely as in PHP or Perl. Somewhat, it errs in being quite full it ends up as unreadable. Ruby tends to assume the intentions of the programmer. This feature begs the question many Ruby students often ask; "How does it know to do that?" In Python, the answer is straightforward; it is merely in its syntax. So, asides being able to enforce indentation for readability, Python also enforces the transparency of information by assuming much less. Since it doesn't assume, Python makes for a smooth variation from the typical way of carrying out things when required while maintaining that the variation remains explicit in the code. By so doing the programmer can do what is necessary while making sure that the code is sensible to those who read it afterward. Usually, after coding with Python, programmers find it quite challenging to switch to other programming languages.

The Upside of Python programming

1. Python has a relatively simple coding system which can be easily read and understood. This feature makes Python a good foundation for kids to learn programming.

2. Python is a productive language. It makes the complicated system of programming more straightforward and reduces the complexity of tasks. Programming is way easier when done in Python than other languages. This characteristic is known as Rapid Application Development (RAD) in computer types.

3. Python is a powerful software with lots of capabilities. Meaning, it can be used to great lengths in diverse fields.

4. Python is a scripting language. There is no compiling system, unlike in other programming languages, so the programs are transferred into Python's interpreter and run. This characteristic makes it relatively faster than other programming languages.

5. Getting feedback on errors is easier and faster on Python, as is detecting and identifying errors. This feature allows a programmer to complete and execute a program more quickly.

6. Python's variables are made from dynamic typing - a piece of big news in the world of programming. Dynamically typed variables make the process of programming easier to carry out because rather than declaring the values of the variables to the program, you can begin using the variable at once.

7. Python enlists the help of many different third-party modules. As such, it is only plausible that those third parties have libraries of their own. A library refers to a collection of codes used for a particular purpose. These

third-party libraries help make programming with Python more straightforward and faster, so one doesn't have to start coding from scratch every other time a new program is being developed. One can use the libraries provided in the program.

8. Unlike other software, Python is free - meaning that the terms of the license for the program respect the freedom of its users.

9. Python can be downloaded and executed for free without any added payments in the future. Thus, one is free to create, own, use, and share a program on the platform without paying a dime. This means that the source code of Python — that is, the human-readable format of the program run by the computer — is available for users. So, anyone can have access to how its developers wrote the program.

Where Python Is Used:

Just about every field of human can use Python. Below are some of the areas python has been applied over time.

- **In space:**

In the development of the central command system for the Robonaut 2 robot, the International Space Station uses Python. Also, in the planned European mission to Mars in 2020, Python would be used to engineer the collection of soil samples.

- **In particle physics labs:**

At the CERN Large Hadron Collider, Python is used in analyzing and deciphering the data obtained from experiments of atom bombardment.

- **In astronomy:**

Python is used in the engineering of the control and monitoring systems in the MeerKat Radio telescope array — the largest radio telescope in the Southern Hemisphere.

- **In movie studios:**

Python is used to automate the process of movie production at the Industrial Light and Magic — the creators of Star Wars. It is also used for the creation of CGI (computer-generated imagery) program, Houdini, at the Side Effects Software which employs Python in programming an interface and for scripting the engine.

- **In games:**

The game company, Activision, uses Python in their programming process for developing, testing, and analyzing games. Activision also uses Python in detecting players who cheat by boosting one another.

- **In the music industry:**

Music streaming services such as Spotify make use of Python to send music to their users.

- **In the video industry:**

Movie service providers such as Netflix use Python to cheat their contents so that movies can be streamed nonstop. YouTube also employs Python in their system.

- **In Internet search:**

In the early stages of Google's development, the search engine giant used Python in their programs.

- **In medicine:**

The Nodality company puts Python to use in managing the data obtained in their search for a cure to cancer.

• In operating systems:

In operating systems such as Linux and Mac OS, Python is used to carry out some administrative functions.

• In home security and automation:

Rupa Dachere and Akkana Peck propose that it is possible to bring a bit of automation into the home using Python to place sensors within a house. With it, one can do tasks such as opening and closing the curtains or blinds, or automatically turning lights on and off when you enter or exit a room.

• How is Python Used?

Python is a programming language which can be used for many purposes. However, most important of all, Python is an interpreted language; meaning that during runtime, its written code isn't converted into a format that is readable by the computer. Whereas, many programming languages require this translation to be done before the program can be run. Programming languages with such qualities were known as scripting language in the past because they were used to carry out trivial tasks. Albeit, this nomenclature changed as a result of Python. The reason being that it is commonplace for large applications to be written almost exclusively in Python in contemporary times.

The application of Python can be used in the following ways:

1. In working with Files

2. In programming CGI for Web Applications

3. In reading from and Writing to PostgreSQL

4. In building RSS Readers

5. In reading from and Writing to MySQL

6. In creating Calendars in HTML

7. Python has a set of widgets of which Tkinter is one of them. These widgets can be used to develop user applications which make use of graphics and not texts alone in interacting with a user.

8. In extending other programs such as GIMP (a 2D photo-retouching program), LibreOffice (office programs), Blender (a 3D modeling program), among others by creating custom scripts.

9. You can create games using graphics via Kivy libraries, Tkinter or Pygames. These games are text-based.

10. The matplotlib can be used in drawing science and math graphs with high complexities.

11. Computer vision can be experimented with using the OpenCV library. Experts in the field of robotics use this feature to provide sights to robots, help them handle things, and help them navigate during motion.

CHAPTER 4: HOW TO LEARN PYTHON

In contemporary times, Python has evolved to become one of the most simple, versatile, and widely used programming languages. In teaching budding programmers, Python is also one of the top-rated options taught across the world. However, the process of learning python isn't quite as easy as it seems what with the many tutorials and books presented online. Worse still, a good many of them appear so dense that a non-programmer can barely make sense of them. In this book, we look to overcome this barrier by putting together contents which are simple to comprehend, but concise. In this section, the focus is directed on how to learn Python. Below are a few steps to take in your journey to python programming.

• **Figure out a reason for learning python:**

In learning Python programming, the primary step to take is figuring out the "why" element. To learn Python and target it towards fulfilling your needs, you have to decipher why exactly you want to learn it. This process is vital in helping you decipher what you would get out of the process and could be your motivation in the long run. It is also helpful in identifying the best way to get started as well as the other necessary skills required for the process.

In finding your 'why,' ponder on the following:

• Why Python?

In learning to code, it is advisable to have a goal in sight during the learning process. Determining the level of skill you want to attain and how you hope to use that skill are vital factors to ponder on in picking a language. Pondering on these should help you decipher if Python is the right programming language for you. Also, you would be able to narrow down your choice of courses to reach your goals. Python, in itself, has its limits, so be sure it is the language that satisfies your needs and goals.

• What plans have you got for learning Python?

If your reason for learning Python is to further a career in programming, you have to take to mind the skills necessary to succeed in your chosen field. For instance, if you want to enter the field of developing back-end web applications using Python, you would have to master skills in web development and framework.

• How much time can you put into the learning process?

Deciphering how much time you can commit to the learning process is an essential factor to consider. The reason is that it is advisable not to take on more responsibilities than one can handle. It is possible to enroll in any course offering Python but making time out to commit to it is critical. If you have a limited amount of time to learn Python, your commitment to the learning process would be limited. Thus, you wouldn't be able to partake in physical classes which clash with your schedule. In this case, an online course is your best bet.

• Use an Interactive Course:

In the world today, interactive learning is the best form of learning python programming. A good many people believe that any other form of learning Python outside interactive courses are a waste of time. And rightly so too.

1. Interactive courses have a host of unique features tailored to the needs of the learner. These features are inclusive but not limited to the following:

2. Interactive courses in coding allow the learners to have a first-hand experience of imputing codes directly into

a browser while staying within the confines of instructions.

3. As the name suggests, when learning through an interactive, one is entitled to regular feedbacks regarding their coding prowess and progress.

4. Interactive courses have a host of levels but start on a smooth note; guiding students up the ladder to more advanced subjects while improving their knowledge reasonably and efficiently.

• **Familiarize yourself with reference guides:**

Regardless of how good you become at coding in Python, there is no mistaking that specific syntax and concepts may be troubling. When you get into such troubles and find it difficult navigating your way out of it, you need to have a book you can look up solutions and necessary information in. Your best choice is a language reference; the reason being that you can quickly and effectively look up things in them. Although there are many different reference guides about Python present today, Python has an official language documentation. This reference guide from Python is more comprehensive than the others and provides more useful and insightful content. So, should you run into an issue or lack a basic knowledge of the syntax, you can look up the Python language reference for solutions.

- **Be around students like yourself:**

While coding might seem like an activity best done alone, it is better when people work as a team. In learning to program with Python, you must surround yourself with people of like mind and intent who are students to the program as well. By doing so, you would have a team to share tips and tricks with during the learning process. Being with such people also means you can seek and get help faster for your programming. If you are seeking a means of meeting people that are interested in Python programming as you are, you can consider searching for local events and meetups near you. There is also a community for python lovers, PythonistaCafe. You can join this group for peer-to-peer learning.

- **Online Networking:**

You can measure how far you have progressed in your programming by connecting to online networks via programming forums and chat boards. For instance, when you are part of an online community, you would become privy to support when you have questions and receive answers readily. In the same vein, you can also try answering other people's questions; in doing this, you are reinforcing your knowledge of the subject.

- **Teach others:**

It is a common saying that the easiest way to learn things is by teaching them. And rightly so, too. In learning python, this Maxim runs true. You can join or create a group or team in which you take turns teaching one another. There are a host of methods to do this. You can host a blog for detailed content on newly acquired concepts in Python, make a podcast or video, or go traditional with the whiteboard. Whichever your pick is, they are helpful strategies which would help strengthen your knowledge and understanding of the subject. Also, you would be able to detect any gaps in your comprehension of the subject and reinforce them.

- **Engage in Pair Programming:**

Pair programming refers to a technique in which two developers share a workstation to carry out a particular task. In this technique, both developers alternate between two roles - the driver and navigator. The driver is in charge of writing the program, while the navigator offers guidance aimed at solving problems, as well as reviewing the written code to eliminate errors. The switching of roles is done to bolster the skills of both developers in the aspects of coding and reviewing. There are tons of benefits associated with pair programming. For one, it affords you the chance to hear a second opinion on a problem, as well as having your coding skills critiqued and your program reviewed. Another benefit is the fact that you would be exposed to several ideologies as well as methods of reasoning, which helps solve problems during solitary coding.

• **Take as many notes as you can:**

In learning any programming language, Python mainly, it is essential for you to take notes. If you are serious about wanting to learn the subject of python programming, you must not be hesitant in taking notes as you progress with the course. Taking notes helps slow down your pace until you can perfectly understandable all the concepts associated with the syntax. By so doing, you won't wind up missing any important details, and all the essential concepts you have learned would be reinforced in your learning faculty. Asides taking notes, you should also consider investing in qualitative texts for beginners in Python programming. Texts of this sort are helpful because you can fall back to them to broaden your knowledge or whenever you need answers.

• Begin developing your codes:

Creating programs of your own is an excellent technique to learn and practice python programming. While it is widely unknown to a great number of beginners, writing programs of your own doesn't necessarily require a lot of skill or experience. You only require a basic understanding of the syntax and features of the python language to be able to build simple blocks of code that can be run. The one thing that can sometimes be a challenge in practicing by creating programs is getting ideas for what to develop. Albeit, it is essential for you to bear in mind that your program needs not necessarily be the next biggest thing. The aim is to be able to write a code block which can be successfully executed without errors. Below is a list of things you can develop using Python:

1. Create a program for an alarm clock which would send a message or notify using sounds at a specific time. Design a simple calculator application.

2. Create a basic script for looking up things on internet webpages.

3. Develop a simple game like tic-tac-toe, number guessing games, or dice roll simulator.

4. Create a notification service for cryptocurrency. All these are but basic applications of Python. You can do more than these, but, again, the point is to be able to string functional blocks of code.

Become a contributor to Open Source:

In the open-source version of Python, the software source code is publicly available to all users; meaning anyone is free to join in the collaboration. A good many Python libraries have their origins in taking contributions from users, as well as from open-source projects. Many organizations publish open-source projects as a means of seeking programmers. In taking up such projects, you would be provided with programs written and produced by the engineers of those organizations. Becoming a contributor to open-source projects in Python can serve as a suitable method of gaining invaluable experience throughout learning.

Say, for instance, you find a bug and turn in a request for a bug fix; you would have to submit a "pull request" to have your fix patched into the code. Afterward, the managers in charge of the project would go through your work and leave suggestions and comments based on their analysis of it. From here, you would be able to learn techniques that work best in python programming and to communicate with fellow developers efficiently.

• Take a break:

As it is with learning anything, it is vital that you momentarily take the time out to absorb everything you have learned. Going on breaks is an essential process to studying effectively and retaining knowledge better, particularly when taking in vast amounts of new knowledge. When debugging, taking a break is especially essential. The reason being that bugs require attention and a great deal of focus to analyze. So, anytime you happen on a bug and can't quite figure it out yet, you may well settle for a break. You can try out the Pomodoro Technique - a method of working for 25 minutes between each break time. Move away from your PC and engage in something recreational like some light stretching for energy, a coffee refill, chatting up a friend, etcetera. In programming, your codes must follow the rules and logic of the language to the letter; otherwise, it would fail to run. Thus, being fresh-eyed and alert is helpful to program right.

• Hunt for bugs:

Just like in real life, bugs also exist in programming; and they are no less liked. It is near impossible to not run into a bug in your code when you begin writing complex programs. However, don't let it get you down; it happens even to the best programmers. Instead, seize these moments to consider yourself somewhat of a bug hunter.

It is necessary to use a methodical approach when attempting to debug, as it is a necessity for identifying places in the code with issues. To do this, you can begin by scanning your codes in the order of execution to ensure every part of it is functional and without any errors. On identifying areas where the issue originates from, you can proceed to use Python's default debugger.

To start the debugging process, enter the line of code below into your script:

import pdb; pdb.set_trace()

Press enter to run. The debugger would take you to an interactive mode from where you can begin debugging the code.

- **Ask many questions:**

Engaging in programming for the first time can be a tad daunting, and you may need to learn the ropes to be able to out Python to productive use. To do this, you would require the help of others, experts, and learners alike. However, to engage their help, you would have to ask questions, regardless of how obvious or silly you think it sounds. Asking questions and receiving answers is one of the easiest ways of learning python programming. Although it can be quite challenging finding someone to direct your questions to, to overcome this hurdle, you would have to surround yourself with other learners or join a forum (online or offline).

Moreover, if it all comes to nothing and you can't get a willing person to answer your questions, you can sign up for a paid learning program in which you are assigned a mentor. Tons of websites offer such services aimed at connecting learners to experts. Not only would they teach you to code, but they would also entertain and reply to your answers in the best way they can.

- **Hack into another person's code:**

Owing to media stereotype, hacking is typically seen as a dirty job done by cybercriminals, but the truth is that hacking isn't necessarily a corrupt activity. There is a form of hacking which is legal and ethical. Since hacking isn't entirely the focus here, we'll leave it at that. To hack means to unpack. That is, you take a code file, or a block of code written by another person, and attempt to unpack it. This process helps learn or reinforce your knowledge of Python. You begin by going through the code file to see the order of execution; this should give you enough knowledge of what each line of code is written to execute. As you go through the program, you can leave comments to help you know certain things you find noteworthy.

Then, you wrap up the process by making improvements in the places you find wanting. If you are wondering whether or not you could get into any legal trouble unpacking other people's programs, then worry no more. There are platforms which provide you with codes to hack. An example is GitHub. All you need do is look up python code files that pique your interest, download it to your PC and run it in a text or code editor like the Atom code editor, or any other of your choosing. Once opened, you can begin going over and working on it.

• How to begin programming with Python

Owing to the relative simplicity of Python in comparison to other programming languages, it's basics can be easily grasped using techniques of trial and error. In this section, we are going to walk you through a process of running basic programs in Python.

• Download python to your PC:

Depending on your operating system, you might need to download the latest version of Python to your system. For PC's running on Windows OS, you can download the Windows Python interpreter from Python's website free of charge. Depending on the version of your operating system, ensure to download the appropriate version of Python that works for it. PCs running on Linux and Mac OS X already have python pre-installed, so you don't have to make any further installing asides a code editor. However, since a good many OS X and Linus systems still run a python 2.x series, you might want to install the newer version of Python. To do this, you have to visit Python's website and download a 3.x series version appropriate for your operating system.

• Install a Python interpreter:

The next step is to install a Python interpreter. Do this without altering any changes to the program. From this point, Python can be integrated into your PC's Command Prompt by activating the last option on the list of available modules.

1. Test the installation by opening the command prompt on Windows and Terminal on Linux or Mac. Enter the word, "python," and click enter. The package would load and display the version number of Python you have installed. From here, the python interpreter command prompt would load. Enter print("Hello, World!") and click enter. The text, "Hello World!" should appear under the python command line.

2. Feel free to experiment with the interpreter. Try out the functionality of codes in the interpreter before adding it to your program. Doing this can aid you in learning the workings of the commands in Python and in being able to write a throw-away program.

3. Learn the basics of how variables and objects are run on Python

4. You can learn to use Python in carrying out simple calculator functions which help familiarize you with the syntax of the program, as well as how strings and numbers are managed.

5. To open the interpreter, visit your Command Prompt center or Terminal. Enter Python into the prompt and click enter to be directed to the Python command prompt. To execute the interpreter, you would have to manually navigate your way to the Python directory if Python isn't already integrated to your Command Prompt.

Use Python to carry out basic arithmetic problems such as addition, subtraction, multiplication, exponent, etcetera. This is done using operators in Python. For instance, to calculate the values of 7^2, 3 + 7, and 5^7. To calculate the following, you enter them into the prompt as follows:

>>> 3 + 7 10

>>> 7 ** 2 # 7 squared

49

>>> 5 ** 7 # 5 to the power of 7

78125

Take note that the interpreter in python programming does not execute the # sign.

• **Try creating your first program:**

You can try creating a program using Python while experimenting with the language. As was earlier mentioned, the program needs not be something big. If anything, it's advisable to start small. So, to begin, open your code editor. You also don't need many skills to get started. All you have to do is write a program, save it, and execute it through the interpreter. Doing this can also serve as a test to affirm that the interpreter was correctly installed.

1. Start by entering a print statement. The print statement is one of the essential features in Python used to display data in the terminal while the program is being run. Print is also one of the advanced features in the Python 3.x series which isn't found in Python 2.x. In Python 2, you would have to enter the words "print" yourself, while python 3 has it as a dedicated function. As such, to use the function, you would have to enter "print()" with what you want to display contained in the parentheses.

2. Add a comment. It is common among programmers to use "Hello World!" as a text to test the functionality of the programming language. Enter the text into the parentheses along with the quotation marks.

3. To save the file, select the File menu of the code editor and click on Save As in the drop-down menu. Just under the name box, click on Python file type. Although it isn't a recommended alternative, when using Notepad, click on "All Files" and proceed to ".py" as a suffix in the file name. Endeavor to save the file in other places as well for ease of access for navigation to the command prompt when needed. For this sample, try saving the file as "hello.py."

4. Execute the program by going to Command Prompt or Terminal and navigating to the location where the file was saved. Once there, highlight the file and click on enter to run. The command prompt should open to display the text, "Hello World!" beneath.

5. Also, depending on the way you installed Python on your PC and the version of Python in use, you may have to enter Python hello.py or python3 hello.py to execute the program.

6. Engage in coding as frequently as possible. Python has no limits to how much practice you can engage in, so feel free to test out any new program of your choosing. You should have your command prompt, and code editor opened at the same time. This way, any changes you save in your code editor can be readily executed as a program in the command prompt. As such, you would be able to test for changes easily and more quickly.

7. Practice coding with some basic flow control statements: A flow control statement lets you take control of how the program responds based on certain conditions. These statements are an integral aspect of python programming as they help you develop programs that respond differently based on what is imputed into it. For example, you can calculate a Fibonacci sequence up to 100 using a statement.

8. Create functions in a program. In Python, you can name a function which can be recalled over time in the program. This feature is particularly helpful when you have to use a variety of functions inside a much bigger program.

9. Learn the basic conditional expressions used with operators. In Python, when determining if an input met a particular condition, a conditional expression is used. Also, although these conditions are similar to the ones found in maths, some are written somewhat differently in Python. For example, in maths, the operators greater than and less than are written as > and < respectively. The operators are written the same way in Python. However, in writing the operators equal to and not equal to, Python is a little different. In maths, they are represented as = and ≠, while in Python they are written as == and !=. To learn more about operators and their uses, see previous chapters.

CHAPTER 5: METHODS

Before we consider python methods, we are going to take a look at methods in a broader sense of computer programming.

In object-oriented programming (OOP), methods refer to a series of procedures affiliated with messages and objects. Objects are made up of behavior and data. In turn, data and behavior consist of an interface which clarifies the way an object is being used by any one of the several users of the object.

Data is identified as the properties of an object while behaviors refer to the methods of an object. For instance, an object in Windows may have methods like "open" and "close," while its state, be it closed or open at any period, would be classified as a property.

Methods are defined in a class in CBP (class-based programming), while objects are examples of a given class. Methods overriding is arguably one of the most critical abilities provided by a method. A single name, for instance, volume, can be used in many different types of classes. This characteristic makes the sending objects capable of executing behaviors and delegating the carrying out of those behaviors to the receiving object. For instance, an object can send an area message to other objects, and regardless of whether the receiving object is a square, circle, rectangle, or triangle, the adequate formula is executed. Methods are useful in providing the interface which other classes use in gaining access to and modifying the data properties of an object. This process is otherwise known as encapsulation. Methods differ from procedure calls as a result of two distinguishing factors, namely, overriding and encapsulation.

Method Overloading and Overriding:

Asides encapsulation, overloading and overriding are two significant ways in which a method is distinguishable from any function call or conventional procedure. Overriding is defined as any subclass that redefines the execution of a method in its superclass. For instance, say, findArea is a method defined on a class of shapes, the several subclasses of this class which include triangle, circle, rectangle, etcetera would determine the formula used in calculating their respective areas.

The general idea is to consider an object as a sort of "black box" such that any alterations in its internal parts are done with little to no effect on other objects which use the box. This is the idea behind encapsulation, meaning it is aimed at making codes easier to be reused and maintained. On the other hand, method overloading is defined as the process of differentiating a code used to manage a message according to the parameters of the method. In the case where the receiving object is considered to be the first parameter of any given method, then overriding is but a particular case of overloading. In this case, however, the selection is based on the first argument alone.

Types of methods

• **Accessor, mutator, and manager methods:**

While accessor methods are used in reading the data values of an object, mutator methods are used in modifying the data contained in an object. Manager methods, on the other hand, are used in signing or destroying the objects in a class, for example, destructors and constructors. These method types offer a layer of abstraction which eases modularity and encapsulation. For instance, if a bank-account class offers a getBalance() accessor method used in retrieving the balance of current accounts instead of directly entering the balance data fields. Over time, revisions of the exact code can execute a more complicated mechanism for balance retrieval like database fetch without having to change the dependent code. Both the concepts of modularity and encapsulation aren't distinct to object-oriented programming (OOP). The object-oriented approach is, in many ways, a logical extension of prior paradigms like structured programming and abstract data types.

• **Constructors:**

Constructors are a type of method which can be invoked at the start of the lifetime of an object — a process known as construction or instantiation. They are used to create and assign the object. Initialization generally includes any process of acquiring resources. Parameters may or may not exist in constructors, but the latter typically doesn't output values in many programming languages.

• **Destructors:**

Destructors refer to any method that is typically invoked automatically at the end period of the lifetime of an object — a process known as destruction. In many programming languages, destruction permits neither return values nor destructor method arguments. Destruction is typically implemented as a process of carrying out cleanup activities as well as other tasks on object destruction.

• Finalizers:

In programming languages such as Python, C#, and Java, which are garbage-collected, destructors are commonly known by the name of finalizers. They are also used for the same purposes and function as destructors. However, owing to the differences between programming languages which have manual memory management and those that use garbage-collection, there is a difference in the sequence in which they are called.

• Abstract Methods:

Abstract methods refer to method types which possess signatures but have no body of implementation. They are commonly used in specifying why a subclass has to offer an implementation of the method. In some programming languages, abstract methods are the types used to specify interfaces.

- **Class methods:**

Class methods can be defined as a method type which is called on a class instead of an instance. Class methods are mainly used as a part of an object meta-model. That is, an object meta-model is created for every class that is defined in an instance. Meta-model protocols allow for the creation and deletion of classes. In this vein, they offer a function quite similar to destructors and constructors. In programming languages like CLOS (Common Lisp Object System), a developer can dynamically change the object model at the time of execution on account of the meta-model. For example, in creating new classes, redefining the class hierarchy, modifying properties, among others.

- **Special Methods:**

Unlike some of the other types of methods, special methods are quite distinct to every programming language. Thus, while one language may be capable of supporting no special method, others may support some or all of them. The compiler in a programming language may generate special methods by default, or a programmer may be granted the allowance to define special methods optionally. Although a good many special methods can't be directly invoked, the compiler is made to generate specific codes with which it invokes them at the right times.

• Static methods:

Of all the types of methods, static methods are defined to have higher relevance in all instances of a class instead of one particular instance. In this sense, static methods share a bit of a likeness to static variables. For instance, a static method can be used to find the sum of values for all the variables available in all instances of a class. Thus, if there was a Product class, static methods could be used in computing the average price of all the products. Owning objects do not exist in static methods, explaining why the latter doesn't run on instances. Instead, static methods obtain all information from their arguments.

• Operator Methods:

Operator methods are used to define or redefine operator symbols, as well as defining the operations which can be carried out using the symbol and the relative method parameters.

Built-in Functions in python programming

The interpreter in Python is equipped with several functions which are almost always handy for use. These functions are known as built-in functions. For instance, the print() function is used to print a specific object to the text stream file or the standard output device like the monitor.

Listed below are the methods in Python programming and their associated functions.

1. Python abs() — Used to return the absolute value of a number.

2. Python all() — Returns as true when all the elements in an iterable are true.

3. Python any() — It checks if any of the Elements of an Iterable are True.

4. Python ascii() — It returns the String Containing Printable Representation.

5. Python bin() — Used to convert integers into a binary string.

6. Python bool() — It converts a specific Value into Boolean.

7. Python bytearray() — Used to return arrays of specific byte size.

8. Python bytes() — Used in returning an immutable bytes object.

9. Python callable() — Used in checking whether or not an Object is Callable.

10. Python chr() — Used to return a Character, usually a string, from an Integer.

11. Python classmethod() — It returns the class method for a specific function.

12. Python compile() — Used to return a Python code object.

13. Python complex() — It is used to create a Complex Number.

14. Python delattr() — Used to delete the attribute from an object.

15. Python dict() — Used in creating a dictionary.

16. Python dir() — Used in attempting to return attributes of an object.

17. Python divmod() Used to return a Tuple of Quotient and Remainder.

18. Python enumerate() — Used to return an Enumerate Object.

19. Python eval() — Used to execute Python codes within the program.

20. Python exec() — Used to run Dynamically Created Programs.

21. Python filter() — Used to construct an iterator from elements that are true.

22. Python float() — Used to return the floating-point number from a number or string.

23. Python format() — It returns a formatted representation of a value.

24. Python frozenset() — It is used to return an immutable frozenset object.

25. Python getattr() — Used to return the value of the named attribute of an object.

26. Python globals() — Used to return the dictionary of the current global symbol table.

27. Python hasattr() — Used to return whether the object has named attribute or not.

28. Python hash() — Used to return the hash value of an object.

29. Python help() — Used in invoking the built-in Help System.

30. Python hex() — Used to convert Integer into Hexadecimal.

31. Python id() — Used in returning the Identity of an Object.

32. Python input() — Used to read and returns a line of string.

33. Python int() — Used in returning an integer from a number or string.

34. Python isinstance() — Used to check if an object is an instance of a Class.

35. Python issubclass() — Used to check if an Object is the Subclass of a Class.

36. Python iter() — Used to return the iterator for an object.

37. Python len() — Used to return the Length of an Object.

38. Python list() Function — Used to create a list in Python.

39. Python locals() — Used in returning the dictionary of a current local symbol table.

40. Python map() — used to apply Function and Returns to a List.

41. Python max() — Used in returning the largest element.

42. Python memoryview() — Used to return the memory view of an argument.

43. Python min() — Used in returning the smallest element.

44. Python next() — Used to retrieve the Next Element from an Iterator.

45. Python object() — used to create a Featureless Object.

46. Python oct() — used in converting integers to octal.

47. Python open() — Used to return a File object.

48. Python ord() — Used in returning the Unicode code point for a Unicode character.

49. Python pow() — Used to return x to the power of y.

50. Python print() — Used in the printing of a specific Object.

51. Python property() — Used to return a property attribute.

52. Python range() — Used in returning a sequence of integers between start and stop.

53. Python repr() — Used to return a printable representation of an object.

54. Python reversed() — Used to return the reversed iterator of a given sequence.

55. Python round() — used in rounding up a floating-point number to n-digits places.

56. Python set() — Used to return a Python set.

57. Python setattr() — Used in setting the value of an attribute of an object.

58. Python slice() — used to create a slice object specified by range().

59. Python sorted() — Used to return a sorted list from a specific iterable.

60. Python staticmethod() — Used in creating a static method from a given function.

61. Python str() — Used to return an informal representation of an object.

62. Python sum() — Used to add the items of an Iterable.

63. Python super() — It allows the user to Refer Parent Class by super.

64. Python tuple() Function — Used in creating a Tuple.

65. Python type() — Used in returning the Type of an Object.

66. Python vars() — Used to return a __dict__ attribute of a class.

67. Python zip() — Used in returning an Iterator of Tuples.

68. Python __import__() — This is an advanced function Called by import.

CHAPTER 6: RUNNING PYTHON SCRIPTS

To excel in Python programming, it is essential for you to have an in-depth knowledge of how to run scripts and code in Python. It is imperative because scripts and codes are the only way with which you can check the functionality of your codes.

So, the key to functional codes lies in being able to run scripts and codes. In this section, the focus is going to be on all the process you can use to run python scripts regardless of the operating system platform, requirements, and skill set you have obtained as a programmer.

To begin, let's consider the concepts of scripts and modules first.

• Scripts and Modules:

In computer programming, a script can be defined as a file which contains a logical sequence of orders. It can also be seen as a batch processing file. It is typically stored in a plain text file as a simple program. To process a script, an interpreter is needed. The interpreter has to run each command sequentially. Thus, any plain text file which contains python codes is known as a script, a term used informally to refer to a top-level program file. However, not all plain text files containing codes in Python are scripts. A module is a plain text file composed of python codes which are designed for importation to another python file from which it is used. Bringing both terms into comparison; a module is distinguishable from a script because while the former is crafted to be imported, the latter are meant to be run directly. Whatever the case may be, the critical thing is to learn how to run the codes you write in Python into your scripts and modules.

• **Interpreter:**

To better understand the concept of scripts and modules, let's delve into the concept of the interpreter. Python can be an interpreter language. An interpreter is a vital program necessary to run python scripts and codes. In technical terms, an interpreter is a form of software which runs the code by working between the hardware of your computer and the program. There are different interpreters spanning across the different types of platforms. Thus, your interpreter can be any of the following depending on the python implementation you use:

1. A program coded in C such as CPython – the core implementation of the programming language.

2. A program coded in Java. For example, Jython.

3. A program coded using python, such as PyPy.

4. A program implemented in .NET. For example, IronPython.

Any code you write would be executed by the interpreter regardless of the form it takes. As such, the primary condition for being able to execute python scripts is to have an interpreter correctly installed in your PC. An interpreter is capable of executing python codes in the following ways;

1. As a block of code entered an interactive session;

2. As a module or script.

• **How python codes are run in interactive session:**

Running python codes via the interactive session is one of the popular ways of executing scripts and modules. To begin the python interactive session, the terminal or command-line is opened. Next, depending on the version of python in use, input the word "python" or "python 3" in and click to enter. The default prompt in the interactive mode is the sign (>>>).

So, whenever you see these characters, keep in mind that you have entered the interactive interface. Here, you can attempt to write and run your python codes. However, as simple as this method seems, it has one major downside: your code lasts as long as the session. Once you terminate your session, your codes are gone. The upside to this method is that any statement and expression you input is immediately evaluated and executed. That it allows you to test each line of code written makes a great tool for development, and a fine platform to practice coding python easily and quickly.

To leave the interactive mode, you could use any other following methods:

1. You can use built-in functions such as exit() or quit().

2. You can also use a combination of keys. For systems with Unix-styled platforms, you can use Ctrl and D. In Windows, on the other hand, you can use the keys, Ctrl + Z and click to enter.

3. Take note that the primary general guideline to keep in mind when coding with python is to use the interactive session when in doubt of the function(s) of any code.

If you have no experience using the terminal or command-line, below are some steps you can use:

1. When using Windows, locate the command-line otherwise known as the MS-DOS console or command prompt. The command-line is a program known as cmd.exe. However, the path to this program can change with the version of your system.

2. To gain quick access to it, you can use the codes Win + R key to get to the Run dialogue. Once the interface opens, input cmd in and click to enter.

3. On platforms that run on GNU or Linux as well as other versions of Unixes, there are numerous applications which provide access to the system command-line. Some of them include Konsole, xterm, Terminal, and Gnome. The tools run terminals or shells such as csh, ksh, Bash, among others. In this scenario, the path to each application is more diverse and is dependent on the way it is distributed, as well as the environment of the PC you use. Hence, it is essential for you to take note of the documentation regarding your system.

4. On systems running on Mac OS X platform, the system terminal is accessible through the following processes;

5. Go to Applications, enter Utilities and click on Terminal.

• **How the interpreter runs python scripts:**

The process of running python scripts is riddled with multiple steps undergone by the interpreter. In doing this, the interpreter does the following:

1. Processing the statements of your script in a manner of sequence.

2. Compiling the source code into bytecode – an intermediate format: The bytecode represents the conversion of the code into a lower-level language which is independent of the platform. The purpose of the bytecode is to optimize the execution of the codes. As such, in running your code, the interpreter boycotts the compilation process. Take note that only modules undergo code mobilization because they are imported, executable scripts don't.

3. Send off the code to be executed: Here, the PVM (Python Virtual Machine) which is the runtime engine

of python is used. The PVM works as a cycle which iterates over the instructions contained in your bytecode, running them one after the other. However, do not consider the Python Virtual Machine to be an isolated part of python. No. It is merely a part of the python system which is installed in your machine. In the Python interpreter, the PVM is the final step.

4. The entirety of the processes required to execute python scripts is referred to as the Python Execution Model.

• How Python Scripts Can be Executed Using the Command-Line:

The interactive session in Python would allow you to write many different lines of code, but the minute you close the window, everything you have written would be lost. This explains why python programs should be written using plain text files. Conventionally, files created this way would be attached with a .py extension which could also be .pyw on Windows operating systems. Any plain text editor can be used in the creation of python codes. To make this section more practical oriented, you would have to create a sample test script to explain how to run a python script.

To begin, open a text editor and enter the following lines of code.

```
1 #/usr/bin/env python3

2

3 print("Hello World!")
```

Proceed to save the file to your directory under the file name, hello.py. This marks the completion of writing your test script.

- **How to use the python command:**

To run your sample python script or any other python script, you would have to use python command. Begin by opening a command-line and entering in the word python 3 or just python depending on your installed version. Next, attach a path to your script in the following fashion:

```
$ python 3 hello.py

Hello World!
```

Click enter to run the script. If your coding is error-free, the execution should work out well, and the words "Hello World!" would be displayed on the screen. So that is how you run a python script. If the script is unable to run, chances are you have made a mistake in your coding or in adding the path, or there might be problems with your installed version of python. Cross-check your text file to ensure it is error-free. If it is, check your path; the way and place the file is saved. If that is also all right, check your python installation. Basically, it is the simplest and most practical way to execute a python script.

- **How to redirect output:**

It is sometimes helpful to save the output of a python script for analysis at a later date. To do that, enter the following line of code:

$ python3 hello.py > output.txt

In doing this, you would redirect the output of the python script to a file named output.txt instead of to stdout — the default system output file. This process is better known as stream redirection and is offered on Unix and Windows supporting platforms. If before now output.txt file doesn't already exist on your system, the procedure would automatically create it. However, if it already exists, the new output would be used to replace the contents in it. Lastly, should you want to add the output from previous other executions to the end of output.txt, endeavor to use two angle brackets (>>) rather than one. Thus, your line of code should be as such:

$ python3 hello.py >> output.txt

Now, instead of being replaced, the output script would be attached to the end of output.txt.

- **How to run modules with the -m option:**

In Python, some command-line options are made available to meet the many different needs of users. For instance, if you want to execute a module in Python, you can run it under the command python -m <module-name>. The function of the -m option is to search the sys.path for a module name whose content runs as __main__.

Take the instance below:

$ python3 -m hello

Hello World!

Take note that the module-name has to be named after a module object rather than a string.

• How to use the Script Filename:

It is now possible to execute a python script by just entering its designated filename where the code is stored into the command prompt. However, this feature is mainly available on the recent version of the Windows OS. The process typically follows this fashion:

C:\devspace> hello.py

Hello World!

The reason this works is that Windows can use the system registry, as well as the file association to find out what program to use in executing the particular file. On systems which support Unix such as GNU or Linux, something akin to that of Windows can also be achieved. Only, here, you would have to input the first line using the following text; #!/usr/bin/env python, in the same way you did with hello.py.

Although this is merely a simple comment for python, the line implies to the operating system the program which must be used in executing the file. The shebang or hash bang (#!) character combo is used to begin the line which continues with the path to the interpreter. There are two methods in which the path to the interpreter can be specified.

They are:

1. #!/usr/bin/python — This line writes the absolute path to the interpreter.

2. #!/usr/bin/env python — This uses the env command of the operating system to locate and run python by locating the PATH environment variable.

The final option is helpful to note because not all systems supporting Unix can locate the interpreter in a similar place. Lastly, to execute such a script, you have to assign permissions for execution to it before entering the filename at the command-line. Below is a sample of how this can be done:

1. $ # Assign execution permissions

2. $ chmod +× hello.py $ # Run the script by using its filename

3. $ ./hello.py

Hello World!

When the hashbang line and the execution permissions are appropriately configured, you would be able to execute the script by just entering its filename into the command-line. In conclusion, you have to keep in mind that if the script isn't contained in the current working directory you are using, this method would be unable to work correctly until the file path is used.

• **Take advantage of import:**

Whenever your module is imported, the real thing that happens is that its contents are loaded for use and access later. One interesting fact about this procedure is that "import" executed the code as its last step.

You may probably be unaware of how the code is executed when a module is made up of variables, classes, constants definition, and functions. However, you would witness a code's execution when the module contains methods, call to functions, among other statements because they generate visible outputs. The "import" option affords you another method of running scripts in Python. Import typically follows after such fashion:

>>> import hello

Hello World!

Keep in mind that this method can only be used once in a session. So, after your first attempt, it is impossible to carry out successive importations even if the content of the module is modified. The reason is that import operations are expensive to execute, and as such, can only be done once. For instance, after your first import, successive attempts would reveal the following:

>>> import hello # Do nothing

>>> import hello # Do nothing again

"Do nothing" appears in both import operations because python acknowledges that the file hello has been imported already.

To be able to run python scripts using import, certain things have to be put in place, such as:

1. The file containing the python code has to be saved in the current working directory in use.

2. The file has to be in the PMSP (Python Module Search Path), where Python searches for the packages and modules you import.

If you don't know what is in the PMSP you currently use, you can find out by running the code below:

>>> import sys

>>> for path in sys.path: ...

print(path)

Executing this code would reveal all the .zip files as well as the list of directories where the program scans the modules you import.

- **How to use imp and importlib:**

importlib refers to a module which provides import_module(). It can be found in the Python Standard Library. It is possible to emulate an import operation using the import_module(), and, thus, run any python script or module. Consider the example below:

>>> import importlib

Importlib.import_module("hello")

Hello World!

<module "hello" from

'/home/username/hello.py'>

Recall that it is impossible to attempt a second import on a module after your first use. Here, importlib.reload() comes in handy in forcing the interpreter to attempt reimportation of the module again. Consider the example below for more clarity:

>>> import hello # First import

Hello World!

>>> import hello # Second import, which does nothing

>>> import importlib

>>> importlib.reload(hello)

Hello World!

<module "hello" from '/home/username/hello.py'>

You must note that the only way this method could work is if the argument of reload() is the name of a module object rather than a string. If a string is used as the argument, reload() would concede a TypeError exception. After modifying a module, importlib.reload() is especially useful if you want to check to see whether your alterations work without exiting your present interactive session. Lastly, for users of the python 2.x series, the reload() function so provided by the module known as imp. importlib.reload() and imp.reload() have similar functions. Consider the sample below:

>>> import hello # First import

Hello World!

>>> import hello # Second import, which does nothing

>>> import imp

>>> imp.reload(hello)

Hello World!

<module "hello" from

'/home/username/hello.py'>

reload() works as a built-in function in the Python 2.x series. It is also added to imp in Python 2.6 and 2.7, to aid the change to python 3.x series. Since the release of python 3.4, imp has been strongly disapproved of in Python. The imppackage now faces pending disapproval as well and could be replaced by importlib.

• How to use runpy.run_path() and runpy.run_module():

runpy is a module included in the Standard Library of python. In it is contained the run_module() which is merely a function that allows a user to execute a module without first importing it. This function returns the globals dictionary of the module that is run. See the example below:

>>> runpy.run_module(mod_name="hello")

Hello World!

{"__name__": "hello",

"_": None}}

The module is found by use of a standard import mechanism and then run on a new module namespace. In this method, the first argument of the run_module() has to be a string bearing the absolute name of the module; that is, without the .py extension.

Also, runpy offers run_path() — which lets the user execute a module by simply entering its place in the filesystem. Consider the example below:

>>> import runpy

runpy.run_path(file_path="hello.py")

Hello World! {"__name__": "<run_path>

", "_": None}}

Similar to run_module(), run_path() also returns the executed module's globals dictionary. For this method to function, the parameter of the file_path have to be a string and can be referred to as the following: The value of any valid entry in the sys.path which contains a __main__ module (__main__.py file) The location of a compiled bytecode file The location of a Python source file

- **How to hack exec():**

In this section, focus in on using exec() to run python scripts and modules. exec() is a built-in function which allows the dynamic execution of a Python code. Unlike the other methods mentioned above, exec() offers an alternative method through which python scripts can be executed.

The steps are explained below:

>>> exec(open("hello.py").read())

"Hello World!"

This line of code opens the hello.py, reads its content, and then forward it to exec(), which finally executed the code. The example above is merely a "hack," which demonstrates the flexibility and versatility of Python.

- **How to use execfile():**

(For python 2.x series only): If your installed python version is of the 2.x series, the execfile() is a built-in function which you can use in executing your python scripts. In execfile(), the first argument must be a string which contains the path of the text file you want to execute.

For instance:

>>> execfile ('hello.py')

Hello World!

In this case, the hello.py is parsed and computed as a series of statements in python.

- **How to Run Python Scripts using a Text Editor or an IDE:**

In the development of applications with more complexity and larger size, the recommended platform for use is a much-advanced code editor or an IDE (Integrated Development

Environment). The reason being that a majority of such programs afford users the chance to execute their scripts while still in the coding environment. It is commonplace to find commands such as Build or Run in the main menu or tool bar of these applications. The standard distribution of python has IDLE (Integrated Development and Learning Environment) listed as its default IDE which can be used for a host of functions inclusive but not limited to debugging, writing, executing scripts and modules, and modification. There are also tons of other IDEs which let a user execute python scripts from the environment. Such IDEs include Eric, Eclipse-PyDev, NetBeans, and PyCharm. There are also text editors with advanced features that let you execute your python scripts. They include Visual Studio Code, Sublime Text, etcetera. To better understand the basics of how to use your preferred text editor or IDE in running your python scripts, take a look at the documentation peculiar to it.

- **How to Run Python Scripts using a File Manager:**

You can run a python script by opening a file manager and double-clicking on its icon. This is arguably one of the least used alternatives in Python programming. Although it isn't widely used in the stages of development, if it is at all used, it can be used when the code is released to be produced.

However, the ability to run your python scripts in two clicks requires some things to be in place for it to work. Certain conditions, depending on the operating system your PC uses, must be satisfied. These conditions include the following:

1. For instance, in Windows, the programs pythonw.e and python.exe are respectively associated with the extensions .pyw and .py. This link between the program and extension is what makes double-clicking capable of executing the script.

2. If the script is one which has a command-line interface, chances are a black window flashing onto your screen is all you would see. However, this can be avoided by adding a statement to the end of the script. The statement should read input("Press Enter to Continue..."). By adding this, you would be able to stop the program by pressing enter. However, keep in mind that this is merely a helpful hack, and has got its drawbacks as well. For instance, if the script contains an error, the execution would terminate before the input() statement is even reached, and no results would be outputted.

3. Being able to run python scripts by double-clicking in the file manager on Unix-like systems is somewhat of a probability.

4. To run it your script has to have the execution permissions, and a bit of help with the shebang hack. So, as was discussed with scripts having command-line interfaces, there might be no outputted results in the screen for you to see. To run python scripts via double-clicking has many inhibitions and is dependent on lots of factors like file manager type, file associations, operating systems, and execution permissions. For this reason, it is a much viable alternative to only use this method when a python script has already undergone debugging and is ready to be produced.

CHAPTER 7: FUNCTIONS IN PYTHON

In Python programming, functions refer to any group of related statements which perform a given activity. Functions are used in breaking down programs into smaller and modular bits. In that sense, functions are the key factors which make programs easier to manage and organize as they grow bigger over time. Functions are also helpful in avoiding repetition during coding and makes codes reusable.

• **The Syntax of Functions:**

The syntax of functions refers to the rules which govern the combination of characters that make up a function. These syntaxes include the following:

1. The keyword "def" highlights the beginning of every function header.

2. A function named is to identify it distinctly. The rules of making functions are the same as the rules which apply for writing identifiers in Python.

3. Parameters or arguments via which values are passed onto a function are optional in Python.

4. A colon sign (:) is used to highlight the end of every function header.

5. The optional documentation string known as do string is used to define the purpose of the function.

6. The body of a function is comprised of one or more valid statements in Python. The statements must all have a similar indentation level, (typically four spaces).

7. An optional return statement is included for returning a value from a function.

Below is a representation of the essential components of a function as described in the syntax.

def function_name(parameters):

'''docstring'''

statement(s)

• **How functions are called in Python:**

Once a function has been defined in Python, it is capable of being called from another function, a program, or the python prompt even. Calling a function is done by entering a function name with a proper parameter.

Docstring: The docstring is the first string which comes after the function header. The docstring is short for documentation string and is used in explaining what a function does briefly. Although it is an optional part of a function, the documentation process is a good practice in programming. So, unless you have got an excellent memory which can recall what you had for breakfast on your first birthday, you should document your code at all times. In the example shown below, the docstring is used directly beneath the function header.

```
>>> greet("Amos")
```

Hello, Amos. Good morning!

Triple quotation marks are typically used when writing docstrings so they can extend to several lines. Such a string is inputted as the __doc__ attribute of the function. Take the example below.

You can run the following lines of code in a Python shell and see what it outputs:

1. >>> print(greet.__doc__)

2. This function greets to

3. the person passed into the

4. name parameter

The return statement:

The purpose of the return statement is to go back to the location from which it was called after exiting a function.

• **Syntax of return:**

This statement is able to hold expressions which have been evaluated and have their values returned. A function will return the Noneobject if the statement is without an expression, or its return statement is itself absent in the function. For instance:

1. >>> print(greet('Amos'))

2. Hello, Amos. Good morning!

3. None In this case, the returned value is None.

CHAPTER 8: STRINGS

In Python, strings are one of the most widely used types. They can be created by placing characters in quotes. In Python, both single quotes and double quotes are treated the same; so, whenever either single or double quotation marks enclose string literals, they are translated the same way.

Thus, "Hello World!" is the same as 'Hello World!'

To create a string is a simple process of providing a variable with a value. Take a look at the example below for more clarity:

varA = "Hello World!"

varB = "Python Programming"

Asides the quotation, string literals can also be displayed using the print() function. For instance:

print('Hello World!')

print("Hello World!")

- **Assigning strings to variables:**

To assign a string to a variable is no different from attaching a value to a variable. The variable name is closely followed by an equal to (=) which precedes the assigned string. See the example for clarity:

If j = 'Hello World!'

print(j)

Hello World!

- **Multiline strings:**

A multiline string can be assigned to a variable using the three quotations (""") or ('''). The reason is that the three quotes imply that the string exceeds a single line.

For example:

(Using three single quotes) j = '''Lorem Ipsum dolor sit amet, consectetur adipiscing élit, sed do eiusmod tempor incididunt ut labore et dolore magna aliqua.'''

print(j)

Or (Using three double quotes) j = """Lorem ipsum dolor sit amet, consectetur adipiscing élit, sed do eiusmod tempor incididunt ut labore et dolore magna aliqua."""

print(j)

In the output, any line break is placed in the same place as in the code.

Features of strings:

• Strings are arrays:

As it is in many different programming languages, strings are also arrays of bytes in Python, which represent Unicode characters. However, since python doesn't have or support any character data type, an individual character represents a string having a length of one. Such a string can also be considered as a substring. In accessing the elements of a string, square brackets [] are used to slice along the indices or index to obtain the substring.

For example:

```
#!/use/bin/python

varA = "Hello World!"
```

varB = 'Python Programming"

print "varA[0]: ", varA[0]

print "varB[1:5]: ", varB[1:5]

In running these lines of code, the following output is produced:

varA[0]: H

varB[1:5]: ytho

• **Slicing:**

The slice syntax can be used in returning a range of characters. To return a part of a string, you ought to state the start and end indexes, separating them using a colon. For instance:

To get the characters between positions 2 and 5 when j is a known variable.

j = 'Hello World!'

Print(j[2:5])

C:\Users\My Name>python demo_string_slicing.py Llo

- **Negative Indexing:**

Negative indexes can be used to begin slicing from the end of a string. See the example for clarity:

To obtain the characters from positions 5 to 1 beginning the count from the end of the string — 'Hello World!' and a variable j.

j = 'Hello World!'

print(j[-5:-2])

C:\Users\My   Name>python demo_string_negativeindex.py orl

- **String Length:**

The len() function is used in obtaining or returning the length of a string.

For example:

j = 'Hello, World!'

print(len(j))

C:\Users\My Name>python demo_string_len.py 13

- **String methods:**

In Python, there are several built-in methods available to use in string operations. They are inclusive but not limited to the following:

1. strip(): This method eliminates any whitespace from the start or end of a string.

For example:

j = ' Hello, World! '

print(j.strip()) # returns 'Hello, World!'

C:\Users\My Name>python demo_string_strip.py Hello, World!

2. lower(): This method is used to return a string to lower case.

For example:

j = 'Hello, World!'

print(j.lower())

C:\Users\My Name>python demo_string_lower.py

hello, world!

124

3. upper(): This is the opposite of the lower() method. It is used in returning a string in capital letters. For example:

j = 'Hello, World!'

print(j.upper())

C:\Users\My Name>python demo_string_upper.py

HELLO, WORLD!

4. replace(): As the name implies, this method is used in replacing one string with another. For instance:

j = 'Hello, World!'

print(j.replace('H', 'Y'))

C:\Users\My Name>python demo_string_replace.py

Hello, World!

5. split(): This method is used in splitting a string into different substrings, provided instances of a separator is found. For instance:

j = 'Hello, World!'

k = j.split(',')

print(j.split(',')) # returns ["Hello", "World!"]

C:\Users\My Name>python demo_string_split.py

["Hello", "World!"]

How To Check Strings

Sometimes, you might need to find a specific character or phrase in a string. It can be quite challenging for multiline strings, hence the need for keywords. So, to find out whether a character or phrase is in a string, two keywords in and not in are used. For example:

Find out if the phrase "fr" is available in the string below:

txt = 'Father Frances fried five fresh fishes for five friends from France'

j = 'fr' in txt

print(j)

C:\Users\My Name>python demo_string_in.py

True

Here's another example to find out whether the phrase "fr" is NOT available in the string below:

txt = 'Father Frances fried five fresh fishes for five friends from France'

j = 'fr' not in txt

print(j)

C:\Users\My Name>python demo_string_not_in.py

False

How To Concatenate Strings:

String concatenation means to combine or merge two strings. To do this, we use operators like the addition (+).

For example:

Concatenate the variables x and y into a variable z.

x = 'Hello'

y = 'World'

z = x + y

print(z)

C:\Users\My Name>python demo_string_concat.py

HelloWorld

You can also take the concatenation process further and introduce a space between the variables. To do this, you add a space in quotes (' '). That is:

x = 'Hello'

y = 'World'

z = x + ' ' + y

print(z)

C:\Users\My Name>python demo_string_concat2.py

Hello World

How To Update Strings:

Already existing strings can be updated by re-assigning their variables to other strings. In this vein, the latest value is still related to the prior value or an utterly new string altogether. For instance:

#!/use/bin/python

varA = "Hello World!"

print 'Updated String :- ', varA[:6] + "Python"

When this line of code is run, the result it outputs is typically in this fashion:

Updated String:- Hello Python

Escape characters:

Escape characters are non-printable characters which can be represented using a backslash notation. In both single and double quotes strings, an escape character maintains the se interpretation. The table below is a list of escape characters used in strings.

1. \a: Represents the alert or bell and is denoted by the hexadecimal character (0×07).

2. \b: Represents backspace and is denoted by the hexadecimal character (0×08).

3. \cx: Represents Control-x and has no hexadecimal character.

4. \C-x: Represents Control-x and has no hexadecimal character.

5. \e: Represents Escape and is denoted by the hexadecimal character (0×1b).

6. \f: Represents Formfeed and is denoted by the hexadecimal character (0×0c).

7. \M-\C-x: Represents Meta-Control-x and has no hexadecimal character.

8. \n: Represents Newline and is denoted by the hexadecimal character (0×1a).

9. \nnn: Represents Octal notation in which n falls within the 0.7 range and has no hexadecimal character.

10. \r: Represents Carriage return and is denoted by the hexadecimal character (0×1d).

11. \s: Represents Space and is denoted by the hexadecimal character (0×20).

12. \t: Represents Tab and is denoted by the hexadecimal character (0×09).

13. \v: Represents Vertical tab and is denoted by the hexadecimal character (0×0b).

14. \x: Represents Character x and has no hexadecimal character.

15. \xnn: Represents the Hexadecimal notation in which n is within the range of a.f, 0.9 or A.F. It has no hexadecimal character.

String special Operators:

Below is a list of special operators used string operations. To promote clarity, an example would be used to explain each operator. For example, take x as a variable for the value "Hello" and y as the variable containing the value "World."

1. Concatenation (+): Used to add the operands on both sides of the operator together. For instance, x + y would equal HelloWorld

2. Repetition (*): Used to create new strings by concatenating several lines of a single string. For example, x*2 would equal HelloHello

3. Slice ([]) :- Used to return a character from a specific index. For example, x[1] would yield.

4. Range Slice [:]: Used to return characters from a specific range. For instance, x[1:4] would yield.

5. Membership (in): Used in returning true for when a character is available in a particular string. For example, H in x would yield 1. That is, True.

6. Membership (not in): Used to return true for when a character isn't available in a specific string. For instance, J not in x would yield 1, i.e., True.

7. Raw String (r/R): Used to suppress the actual meanings of escape characters. Raw strings have a similar syntax to normal strings, except for the presence of the letter "r" — the raw string operator — which comes before the quotes. The raw string operator can either be in lowercase (r) or uppercase (R) and has to be positioned directly before the first quotation mark. For example, print R"\n" prints \n as does r"\n."

8. Format (%): Used for carrying out string formatting. Examples can be found in the next header.

String Format Operator:

The string Format operator (%) is arguably one of the fanciest features in Python. The operator shares a uniqueness to string and makes up for sharing functions with the print() family in C. For example:

```
#!/use/bin/python
```

```
print 'My name is %s, and weight is %d kilograms!' % ("Amos", 25)
```

When this line of code is executed, the following is outputted:

'My name is Amos and weight is 25 kilograms.

Below is a complete list of symbols which can be combined with the format operator:

1. %c: To convert into character.

2. %s: To make string conversion through str() before formatting is done.

3. %i: To convert into signed decimal integers.

4. %d: To convert into signed decimal integers.

5. %u: To convert into unsigned decimal integers.

6. %o: To convert into octal integers.

7. %x: To convert into lowercase hexadecimal integers.

8. %X: To convert into uppercase hexadecimal integers.

9. %e: To convert exponential notations with a lowercase "e."

10. %E: To convert exponential notations with an uppercase "E."

11. %f: To convert into a floating-point real number.

12. %g: To convert into the shorter form of %f and %e

13. %G: To convert into the shorter form of %f and %E.

There are also many symbols supported by the format operator with different functionalities. They are:

1. (*): The argument indicates precision or width.

2. (-): Stands for left justification.

3. (+): Used to display the sign.

4. (<sp>): Used to leave the space before a positive number blank.

5. (#): Used to add the hexadecimal leading 'OX' or 'Ox', or Octal leading "0" (zero) depending on the use of either 'X' or 'x.'

6. (0): Used to pad towards the right with zeros rather than spaces. (%): "%%" yields only a single literal "%." (var): Used as a mapping variable (dictionary elements).

7. (m.n.): m refers to the minimum total width while n represents the number of digits which is displayed after a decimal point when applied.

String Constants:

String constants refer to the identifiers which are bound to a fixed value and have been named to promote readability of source code. Some of the string constants used in Python include the following:

1. string.ascii_letters: This constant refers to the concatenation of the ascii_uppercase and ascii_lowercase. Its value isn't locale-dependent.

2. string.ascii_lowercase: This constant indicates the lowercase letters a to z. It is also not subject to change or locale-dependent.

3. string.ascii_uppercase: This constant indicates the lowercase letters A to Z. It is also not subject to change or locale-dependent.

4. string.digits: This constant refers to the string of numbers from 0 to 9.

5. string.hexdigits: This constant refers to the string of numbers and letters: "0123456789abcdefABCDEF."

6. string.letters: This constant refers to the concatenation of uppercase and lowercase strings. The specific value of this constant tends to be updated whenever locale.setlocale() is called, making it locale-dependent.

7. string.lowercase: This constant refers to a string comprised of all the characters in the array of lowercase letters. It appears in many systems and the string "abcdefghijklmnopqrstuvwxyz." The specific value of this constant tends to be updated whenever locale.setlocale() is called, meaning it is locale-dependent.

8. string.octdigits: This constant refers to the string of numbers between 0 and 7; "01234567." string.punctuation: This constant refers to a string of ASCII characters that are identified as punctuation characters in the Clocale.

9. string.printable: This constant refers to a string of characters which can be printed. It is usually a

combination of whitespace, letters, punctuation, and digits.

10. string.uppercase: This constant is a string comprising of all the characters which are identified as uppercase letters. It appears in many systems and the string "ABCDEFGHIJKLMNOPQRSTUVWXYZ." The specific value of this constant tends to be updated whenever locale.setlocale() is called, meaning it is locale-dependent.

11. string.whitespace: This constant refers to a string comprising of all characters identified as whitespace. In many systems, it includes such characters like vertical tab, linefeed, tab, formfeed, space, and return.

What is a string module?

A string module comprises of several useful classes and constants, as well as some out of favor legacy functions which are also in use as methods on strings. Also, the built-in string classes in Python support the sequence type methods such as xrange section, str, buffer, list, Tuple, Unicode, as well as string-specific methods.

Unicode String:

While strings in Unicode are stored as 16-bit Unicode, in Python, normal strings are internally stored as an 8-bit ASCII. This feature makes for a more diverse array of characters, even special characters from many other programming languages. When the code below is run:

#!/use/bin/python

print u"Hello, World!"

The result is as follows:

Hello, world!

As can be seen in this string, Unicode, denoted by the "u," was used as a prefix in the code; in a similar way to how r is used in raw strings.

Built-in String Methods:

In Python, there are a number of built-in methods used in the manipulation of string operations. Such methods are inclusive but not limited to the following:

1. capitalize(): This method is used in capitalizing the beginning letter of a string.

2. center(width, fillchar): This method is used to return a space-padded string with the initial string centered to a number of width columns.

3. count(str, beg= 0,end=len(string)): This method is used in counting the number of times str appears in a string or in the substring of a string when a beginning index 'beg' and ending index 'end' is available.

4. decode(encoding='UTF-8',errors='strict'): This method is used in decoding a string by means of code registered for the purpose of encoding defaults into the string encoding.

5. encode(encoding='UTF-8',errors='strict'): This method is used in returning the encoded string version of a string. In the happenstance of an error, ValueError would be raised by default unless errors are offered with "replace" or "ignore."

6. endswith(suffix, beg=0, end=len(string)): This method defines whether the index of a string or its subscript is terminated by a suffix when the starting index beg and the ending index end add specified. If so, it returns true and false when otherwise.

7. expandtabs(tabsize=8): This method is used in expanding the tabs in a string into multiple spaces, and defaults into 8 spaces for each tab if no tab size is specified.

8. find(str, beg=0 end=len(string)): This method is used in determining whether str occurs in a substring or string when the starting and ending index (beg and end) are provided, returns the index if obtained, otherwise -1.

9. index(str, beg=0, end=len(string)): This method is the same thing as the find() function. However, it raises an exception when str isn't found.

10. isalnum(): This method is returned as true when a string contains about one number while the other characters are alphabetic and thus, false.

11. isalpha(): This method returns as true when a string contains at least one character when all characters are alphabetic; otherwise, it reads false.

12. isdigit(): This mode returns as true when a string is comprised of only digits; otherwise, it reads false.

13. islower(): This method returns as true when a string has at least one of its characters cased, and all its characters are in lowercases. Otherwise, it is false.

14. isnumeric(): This method returns as true when a Unicode string comprises numeric characters alone; otherwise, it is false.

15. isspace(): This method returns as true when a string comprises of only whitespace characters and is false otherwise.

16. istitle(): This method returns as true when a string is adequately "titlecased." Otherwise, it is false.

17. isupper(): This method returns as true when a string contains at least a single cased character, and all its cased characters are uppercases. Otherwise, it is false.

18. join(seq): This method combines (as in concatenation) a string's representation of elements in the sequence (seq) into a string using a separator string.

19. len(string): This method returns the length of a string.

20. ljust(width[, fillchar]): This method returns a space-padded string having the initial string left-justified to a total of width columns.

21. lower(): This method is used in converting all letters of a string in uppercase to lowercases.

22. Istrip(): This method is used in removing all the leading whitespace present in a string.

23. maketrans(): This method is used in returning a translation table meant for use in the translate function.

24. max(str): This method is used in returning the max alphabetical character from a string (str).

25. min(str): This method is used in returning them in alphabetical character from a string (str).

26. replace(old, new [, max]): This method is used in replacing all the occurrences of an old in a string with new, or at most max occurrences should max be given.

27. rfind(str, beg=0,end=len(string)): This method is similar to find(), but is used to search a string backwards.

28. rindex(str, beg=0, end=len(string)): This method is similar to index(), but is used to search a string backwards.

29. rjust(width,[, fillchar]): This method returns a space-padded string having the initial string right-justified to a total of width columns.

30. rstrip(): This method is used in removing any trailing whitespace in a string.

31. split(str="", num=string.count(str)): This method is used to split a string in accordance with the delimiter str with space if not given and return a list of substrings. Splitting is done into the most num of substrings if specified.

32. splitlines(num=string.count('\n')): This method is used to split strings at num or all NEWLINan, returning a list of each line that has NEWLINEs removed.

33. startswith(str, beg=0,end=len(string)): This method is used to determine whether a string or the substring of a string (if its beginning index beg and ending index end are specified) begin with a substring str, and if so returning true, and otherwise false.

34. strip([chars]): This method is used to perform both rstrip() and Istrip() functions on a string.

35. swapcase(): This method is used to invert cases for all the letters in a string.

36. title(): This method is used to return a "titlecased" version of a string, that is, all the words start with an uppercase letter while the rest are in lowercases.

37. translate(table, deletechars=""): This method is used in translating strings in accordance with the translation table str(256 chars), taking out those occupying the del string.

38. upper(): This method is used to convert letters in lowercases in a string into uppercase.

39. zfill (width): This method is used to return an original string left-padded with zeros to a total of width characters. As meant for numbers, zfill() holds any given sign less than one zero.

40. isdecimal(): This method returns as true when a Unicode string is made up of decimal characters alone. Otherwise, it is false.

CHAPTER 9: EXAMPLES OF CODING

To become better at python programming, practicing to code is one of the best methods of achieving success. The process of practicing would help reinforce your knowledge of the language, as well as giving you a first-hand experience in the process. So far, the most common program you have created and executed using python is the "Hello World!" script. However, there is more to writing codes than just that. So, in this section, we are going to cover many different examples of coding you can try out as a beginner.

• **CommandLineFu using Python:**

In this example, we are going to create a program using an already existing API from CommandLineFu.com. Whenever you want to write a code for web-based services, it is crucial you ascertain whether or not they have an API. CommandLineFu is the pick for this example because they have an API, and the content they provide comes in many different formats which can be manipulated in different ways.

Webpages that contain lists of commands like listings by user, tag or function, can be translated into any desired format by simple alteration of the request URL.

The test URL provided for this example is:

http://www.commandlinefu.com/commands/'command-set'/'format'/

Where:

1. Command-set refers to the component of the URL representing the set of commands that would be returned.

2. Format refers to one of these; rss, json or plaintext.

3. For this example, the json format is used.

The possible return values include the following:

1. matching/ssh/c3No

2. tagged/163/grep

3. browse/sort-by-votes

How To Begin Creating The Command Line Search Tool

All the necessary API information is handy, so we can now begin creating our program. The program is simplified and concise, so it should be relatively easy to follow.

1. Begin by opening your code editor and enter in the lines of code written below:

```
#!/use/bin/env.python27

import urllib2

import base64

import json

import os

import sys

import re

os.system('clear')

print '-' * 80

print 'Command Line Search Tool'
```

```python
print '-' * 80

def Banner(text):

print '=' * 70

print text

print '=' * 70

sys.stdout.flush()

def sortByVotes():

Banner("Sort By Votes")

url = 'http://www.commandlinefu.com/commands/browse/sort-by-votes/json'

request = urllib2.Request(url)

response = json.load(urllib2.urlopen(request))

#print json.dumps(response.indent=2)

for c in response:

print '-' * 60
```

```
print c["command"]

def sortByVotesToday():

Banner("Printing All commands the last day (Sort By
Votes)")

url =
'http://www.commandlinefu.com/commands/browse/las
t-day/sort-by-votes/json'

request = urllib2.Request(url)

response = json.load(urllib2.urlopen(request))

for c in response:

print '-' * 60

print c["command"]

def sortByVotesWeek():

Banner("Printing All commands the last week (Sort By
Votes)")

url                                              =
'http://www.commandlinefu.com/commands/browse/las
t-week/sort-by-votes/json'
```

```python
request = urllib2.Request(url)

response = json.load(urllib2.urlopen(request)

for c in response:

print '-' * 60

print c["command"]

def sortByVotesMonth():

Banner("Printing All commands the last month (Sort By Votes)")

url = 'http://www.commandlinefu.com/commands/browse/last-month/sort-by-votes/json'

request = urllib2.Request(url)

response = json.load(urllib2.urlopen(request)

for c in response:

print '-' * 60

print c["command"]

def sortByVotesMatch(): #import base64
```

```python
Banner('Sort By Votes')

match = raw_input('Please enter a search command: ')

bestmatch = re.compile(r" ")

search = bestmatch.sub("+", match)

b64_encoded = base64.b64encode(search)

url =
'http://www.commandlinefu.com/commands/matching/'
+ search + '/' + b64_encoded + '/json'

request = urllib2.Request(url)

response = json'.load(urllib2.urlopen(request))

for c in response:

print '-' * 60

print c["command"] print "'"
```

1. Sort By Votes (All time)

2. Sort By Votes (Today)

3. Sort By Votes (Week)

4. Sort By Votes (Month)

5. Search for a command

Press enter to quit

```python
while True: answer = raw_input('What would you like to do?
')

if answer == '':

sys.exit()

elif answer == '1':

sortByVotes()

elif answer == '2':

print sortByVotesToday()

elif answer == '3':

print sortByVotesWeek():

elif answer == '4':

print sortByVotesMonth():

elif answer == '5':
```

```
print sortByMatch()
```

```
else:
```

```
print 'Not a valid choice'
```

Proceed to save the file under the name "commandlinefu.py," and exit the code editor.

When you execute the program, a menu would be displayed to you from which several choices can be made to output different outcomes. It would be something of this fashion:

Command Line Search Tool

----

1. Sort By Votes (All time)

2. Sort By Votes (Today)

3. Sort By Votes (Week)

4. Sort By Votes (Month)

5. Search for a command Press enter to exit What would you like to do? ...

• Port Scanner In Python:

This example covers a step by step guide on how to create a small and relatively easy-to-use port scanner program using python. Although there are diverse methods of doing this, we are going to be using the built-in python socket module. The socket module in Python allows a user to access the BSD socket interface. It is comprised of the socket class used in handling the real data channel, and functions for tasks related to network like changing the name of a server to an address and formatting the data to be communicated throughout the network. In the internet, sockets are a widely used phenomenon because they form the background of any form of network communication done by a system. The INET sockets are responsible for a substantial percentage (almost 99% as of 2013) of all sockets used in the world. Any web browser you use has an assigned socket it opens to connect to a web server. As a matter of fact, every network connection passes through a socket.

Socket Functions:

Before we delve into writing the codes for the port scanner, let us take a look at the different sockets we would be using. They include the following:

1. sock = socket.socket (socket_family, socket_type): This is the syntax for the creation of a socket.

2. sock = socket.socket (socket.AF_INET, socket.SOCK_STREAM): This function is used to create a stream socket.

3. AF_INET: The Socket Family (for this example Address Family version 4 or IPv4)

4. SOCK_STREAM: The Socket type TCP connections.

5. SOCK_DGRAM: The Socket type UDP connections.

6. gethostbyname('host): This function translates the host name into an IPv4 address format.

7. socket.gethostbyname_ex('host): This function translates the host name into an IPv4 address format with an extended interface.

8. socket.getfqdn("8.8.8.8"): The function to get the fqdn (a fully qualified domain name).

9. socket.gethostname(): The function used in returning the hostname of the machine.

10. socket.error: This is a function for exception handling.

How To Make A Program With Python Sockets:

Having learned the essential functions to use, we will now turn our attention to applying them to make a port scanner program using python sockets. When created, the port scanner program would attempt to connect to every port defined to a specific host. To begin, you need to import the python socket library as well as other vital libraries needed for the process.

Proceed to open a code editor and enter in the lines of code written below:

#!usr/bin/env python

import socket

import subprocess import sys

From datetime import datetime

Clear the screen

subprocess.call("clear", shell=True)

Ask for output

remoteServer ,= raw_imput('Enter a remote host to scan: ')

```
remoteServerIP = socket.gethostbyname(remoteServer)

# Print a cute banner with information on which host we are
about to scan.

print '-' * 60

print '

Please wait, scanning remote host', remoteServerIP

print '-' * 60

# Check what time the scan began

t1 = datetime.now() #

Using the range function to specify ports (here it would scan
every port between 1 and 1024)

# We also put in some error handling for catching errors

try:

for port in range(1,1025):

sock = socket.socket(socket.AF_INET,
socket.SOCK_STREAM)

result = sock.connect_ex((remoteServerIP, port))
```

```python
if result == 0:

print 'Port {}: Open'.format(port)

sock.close()

except Keyboardinterrupt:

print 'You pressed Ctrl+C'

sys.exit()

except socket.gaierror:

print "Hostname could not be resolved. Exiting"

sys.exit()

except socket.error:

print 'Could not connect to server'

sys.exit()

# Checking the time again

t2 = datetime.now()

# Calculates the difference of time to see how long it took to
execute the script
```

total = t2 - t1

Printing the information to screen

print "Scanning Completed in: ", total

Once you are done writing the code, save to file under the name "portscanner.py." Proceed to exit the code editor. Once you execute the program, the output should take after such fashion showed below:

$ python portscanner.py

Enter a remote host to scan: www.your_host_example.com

Please wait, scanning remote host xxxx.xxxx.xxxx.xxxx

Port 21: Open

Port22: Open

Port 23: Open

Port 80: Open

Port 110: Open

Port 111: Open

Port 143: Open

Port 443: Open

Port 465: Open

Port 587: Open

Port 993: Open

Port 995: Open

Scanning Completed in: 0:07:35.701507

Take note that the purpose of this program is for people to test for weak security in their equipment; no responsibility would be taken by the author should this program be put to other uses besides this.

• Program to obtain WHOIS information using pywhois

Before we delve into this example, let's take a look at what pywhois is. Pywhois refers to a module in python used in retrieving the WHOIS information of domains. It is usually workable on python 2.4 and has no dependencies on external elements. To install pywhois, you have to do it using the pop command. So, pip installs python-whois, once completed, begin writing your program. However, keep in mind that it is important you import it before beginning.

So, your first lines of code should be something of this sort:

>>> import whois

The pywhois module is typically used in directly querying a WHOIS server, and parsing WHOIS data for a specific domain. Therefore, it is highly possible to obtain data for all the widely used TLDs such as org, net, com, among others. Pywhois has a project website were detailed steps on how to extract data using pywhois is published. To begin creating this sample program, you first import the WHOIS module as mentioned earlier. Next, you assign it a variable as follows:

>>> import whois

>>> w = whois.whois("pythonforbeginners.com")

Enter the following to print the values of every attribute that is found attribute:

>>> print w

The output should be similar to the one outlined below:

creation_date: [datetime.datetime(2012, 9, 15, 0, 0), "15 Sep 2012 20:41:00"]

domain_name: ["PYTHONFORBEGINNERS.COM", pythonforbeginners.com"]

updated_datw: 2013-08-20 00:00:00

whois_server : whois.enom.com

This can be printed out as any attribute of your choice.

If, for instance, you want to print out only the expiration date.

>>> w.expiration_date

Display the content obtained from the WHOIS server

>>> w.text

You can promote how interactive the program can be with users by adding a prompt for users to input any domain of their choice and get the WHOIS data for it.

import WHOIS

data = raw_input('Enter a domain: ')

w = whois.whois(data)

print w

The pywhois module from python allows us the permissions to do lookups on WHOIS using python.

- **Google Command-line Script:**

This example is all about using python in creating a Google command-line script. The python version used for this example is the 2.7 version. To be able to import the modules required for this example, you would have to make a request to the API of the web search. The modules required are listed below:

urllib2: Used to load the URL response.

urllib: To use the urlencode.

json: Google can return JSON.

The next step is to highlight the specific URL for which the request would be directed to:

http://ajax.googleapis.com/ajax/services/search/web?v=1.0&

To promote user interaction with the program, the program would request the user for specific inputs which would be saved to a variable under the name of "query."

Thus;

query = raw_input('What do you want to search for ? >> ')

To create the response object, you need to load the URL response, as well as the query asked of the user above.

response = urllib2.urlopen (url + query).read()

Process the JSON string.

data = json.laods (response)

At this juncture, feel free to experiment with the results as you want. The complete script containing all the processes is shown below:

import urllib2

import urllib2

import json

```
url =
'http://ajax.googleapis.com/ajax/services/search/web?v=
1.0&'

query = raw_input('What do you want to search for ? >> ')

query = urllib.urlencode( {"q" : query } )

response = urllib2.urlopen (url + query ).read()

data = json.loads ( response )

results = data [ "responseData" ] [ "results" ]

for result in results:

title = result["title"]

url = result["url"]

print ( title + "; " + url )
```

Enter the following lines of code into your code editor. Proceed to save the file under the name GoogleSearch.py and leave the editor environment.

When you execute the script, you should see something similar to this:

$ python searchGoogle.py

What do you want to search for ! >> python for beginners

BeginnersGuide – Python Wiki:

http://wiki.python.org/moin/BeginnersGuide

Python For Beginners:

https//www.python.org/about/gettingstarted/

Python For Beginners:

https://www.pythonforbeginners.com/

• Hangman Game in Python

The hangman game is a classic across all levels of gaming, and python had its own very script for it. As usual, there is a series of dashes representing letters of a word to be guessed by the player. If the player guesses a letter correctly that can be found in the word, the script places the letter into its rightful position. A player has ten turns per round to make a correct guess at the word. However, in recreating the game, feel free to change the variables as you want.

Below is the hangman script in Python:

```python
#importing the time module

import time

#welcoming the user

name = raw_input('What is your name? ')

print 'Hello, ' + name, 'Time to play Hangman' print '

#wait for 1 second

time.sleep(1)

print 'Start guessing...'

time.sleep(0.5)

#here we set the secret #creates a variable with an empty value

Guesses =

"#determine the number of turns

turns = 10

# Create a while loop

#check if the turns are more than zero
```

```python
while turns > 0:

    # make a counter that starts with zero

    failed = 0

    # for every character in secret_word

    for char in word:

        # see if the character is in the players guess

        If char in guesses:

            # print then out the character

            print char,

        else:

            # if not found,

            print a dash print '_',

            # and increase the failed counter with one

            failed += 1

    # if failed is equal to zero

    # print You Won
```

```
If failed == 0:

Print

" You won"

# exit the script

Break

Print

# ask the user to guess a character

guess = raw_input('guess a character:')

# set the players guess to guesses += guess

# if the guess is not found in the secret word

if guess not in word:

# turns counter decreases with 1 (now 9)

Turns -= 1

# print wrong

print 'wrong

# how many turns are left
```

```python
print 'You have', + turns, "more guesses"

# if the turns are equal to zero

If turns == 0:

# print 'You Lose'

print 'You Lose'
```

- **Date and Time Script:**

This program is used in parsing date and time. To begin, create a blank file and save it under the name of dateParser.py. Next, enter the following strings of code into the file

```python
from datetime import datetime

now = datetime.now()

mm = str(now.month)

dd = str(now.day)

yyyy = str(now.year)

hour = str(now.hour)

mi = str(now.minute)
```

ss = str(now.second)

print mm + '/' + dd + '/' + yyyy + ' ' + hour + ':' + mi + ':' + ss

Proceed to save the file before exiting. To execute the file, run it using

$ python dateParser.py

Time.sleep:

The time.sleep() function is used in Python to hold off the execution for a specific amount of seconds. The seconds are specified between parenthesis.

How to sleep for 0.5 seconds in Python:

import time

time sleep (0.5)

How to obtain the present time and dat

import datetime

Now = datetime.datetime.now()

Print

print 'Current date and time using the str method of datetime object:'

print str(now)

print

print 'Current date and time using instance attributes:' print 'Current year: %d' % now.year

print 'Current month: %d' % now.month

print 'Current day: %d' % now.day

print 'Current hour: %d' % now.hour

print 'Current minute: %d' % now.minute

print 'Current second: %d' % now.second

print 'Current microsecond: %d' % now.microsecond

print print 'Current date and time using strftime;'

print now.strftime('%Y-%m-%d %H:%M')

The result would typically be something of this sort: When using the str method of datetime object, current date, and time would be: 2019-08-11 20:59:47:38317 When using instance attributes, current time and date would be:

Current year: 2019

Current month: 8

Current day: 11

Current hour: 20

Current minute: 59

Current second: 47

Current microsecond: 383175

When using string, current time and date would be:

2019-08-11 20:49

• Making a bitly shortened using Python

Bitly lets people shorten and share URLs, as well as tracking links. It is a great way to discover, share, and save URLs across the internet. Bitly offers APIs to the public intended at making it relatively more comfortable to be put to use by Python programmers.

You can begin by visiting Bitly at dev.bitly.com where the documentation for the APIs is located, as well as the code libraries, best practices, public data, among others. However, what makes API so crucial in this example? An API key is a necessary component for almost all social media networks such as Twitter and Facebook. API key is an acronym for application programming interface key. The API key refers to a code passed in using computer programs which call an API to specify the identity of the calling program, who developed it, and the user on the website. The use of API keys is to keep track and manage the way and manner an API is used. For instance, abuse or malicious use of the API can be curtailed using API keys.

API keys serve multiple functions, so, asides being a secret token used in the authentication, it is also a unique identifier. Beyond these characteristics, the API key has a series of access rights over the API it is assigned to. The second step is to obtain a Bitly API key.

To be granted permission to shorten links on the platform, you have to sign up and be given an API key. There isn't much to the signing up process asides the basics, so it is pretty straightforward.

Libraries in Bitly code:

There are several developers who have developed code libraries aimed at interacting with the bitly. There are many different languages, and they all contain APIs. Also, since programming is done mainly in Python, it is essential that we know how python libraries work.

To begin the programming process, you start by installing the Bitly API, which is a relatively straightforward process.

installation with PIP

Pip install bitly_api

Downloading/unpacking bitly-api

Downloading bitly-0.2.tar.gz

Running setup.py egg_info for package bitly-api

Installing collected packages: bitly-api

Running setup.py install for bitly-api

Successfully installed bitly-api Cleaning up..

How to shorten a URL:

The script being created is one which decreases the length of an URL to make for easier sharing. To begin, open your code editor and enter the strings of code shown below:

```python
#!/usr/bin/env python

# import the modules

import bitlyapi

import sys

# Define your API information

API_USER = 'your_api_username

API_KEY = 'your_api_key'

b = bitlyapi.BitLy(API_USER, API_KEY)

# Define how you use the program usage = '''

Usage: python shortwner.py [url]

e.g python shortener.py http://www.google.com'''

if len(sys.argv) != 2:
```

print usage

sys.exit(0)

longurl = sys.argv[1]

response = b.shorten(longUrl=longUrl)

print response ["url"]

Proceed to save the script under the name "shortener.py."

How the shortener.py works:

Recall that the program started with the line:

#!/use/bin/env python

Next, the modules required to write the program were imported:

import bitlyapi

import sys

Then the API information was defined:

API_USER = 'your_api_username

API_KEY = 'your_api_key'

b = bitlyapi.BitLy(API_USER, API_KEY)

Moreover, we defined how the program is to be used:

usage = '''Usage: python shortwner.py [url]

e.g. python shortener.py http://www.google.com'''

if len(sys.argv) != 2:

print usage

sys.exit(0)

We created a variable longurl and set a value for the argument entered:

longurl = sys.argv[1]

The longurl is then fed into the Bitly API:

response = b.shorten(longUrl=longUrl)

Then finally, the URL value is printed:

print response ["url"]

• Sending Emails with Python:

There are several modules in Python's standard library regarding working with email servers and emails in general. For this example, we would be using the smtplib module.

A smtplib module is one which specified an SMTP client session object which can be used to forward mail(s) to any internet machine that has an ESMTP or SMTP listener daemon. SMTP is an acronym for Simple Mail Transfer Protocol. The smtplib modules come in handy when communication with mail servers to send mail is needed. To send a mail with smtplib in Python, an SMTP server is used. The complexity of an email, as well as the email server's settings influence the sending process, such that, actual usage tends to vary. The details for this example are based on sending emails through Google mail (Gmail).

Below is a detailed step by step guide on what to enter in your code editor:

'''The first step is to create an SMTP object, and each object is used to connect with one server.'''

import smtplib

server = smtplib.SMTP("smtp.gmail.com", 586)

```python
#Next, log in to the server

server.login('youremailusername', 'password')

#Send the mail

msg =

' Hello!' #The /n separates the message from the headers

server.sendmail('you@gmail.com',    'target@example.com',
msg)
```

We would have to introduce From, To and Subject headers, but smtplib is unable to modify the content or header to any degree. So, to do this, we would use the email package instead. The email package in Python is comprised of many different functions and classes for creating and parsing email messages. To begin using the email classes, we first have to import all the essential classes necessary for the process — saving us time from having to use a full module name afterward. So:

```python
from email.MIMEMultipart

import MIMEMultipart from email.MIMEText
```

import MIMEText Next, we begin composing some of the common message headers:

fromaddr = 'you@gmail.com'

toaddr = 'target@example.com'

msg = MIMEMultipart()

msg["From"] = fromaddr

msg["To"] = toaddr

msg["Subject"] = 'Python email'

The next thing to add is the body of the mail to the MIME message:

body = 'Python test message'

msg.attach(MIMEText(body, "plain"))

To send the mail it is important that we convert the object to a string, and use the same steps as shown above to send the mail with the SMTP server:

import smtplib

server = smtplib.SMTP("smtp.gmail.com", 587)

```
server.ehlo()

server.starttls()

server.ehlo()

server.login('youremailusername', 'password')

Text = msg.as_string()

server.sendmail(fromaddr, toaddr, text)
```

How to verify an email address:

To check the validity of the entered email address, the SMTP protocol is equipped with a command designed to check the server for it. Usually, the VRFY button is disabled to limit spamming from spammers getting legitimate email accounts. However, if it is enabled, you can verify the status of an address using the server and get a status report indicating the validity as well as the full name of the holder. For example:

```
import smtplib

server = smtplib.SMTP("mail")

server.set_debuglevel(True) # show communication with the
server
```

```
try:

dhellmann_result = server.verify("dhellmann")

notthere_result = server.verify("notthere")

finally:

server.quit()

print "dhellmann:", dhellmann_result

print "notthere :", notthere_result
```

How to send emails using Google mail (Gmail):

```
import smtplib

def sendemail(from_addr, to_addr_list, cc_addr_list)

subject, message,

login, password,

smtpserver="smtp.gmail.com:587"):

header = "From: %s "

% from_addr

header += "To: %s
```

```
" % "," .join(cc_addr_list)

header += "Cc: %s

" % "," .join(cc_addr_list)

header +=

"Subject: %s " % subject

message = header + message

server = smtplib.SMTP(smtpserver)

server.starttls()

server.login(login.password)

problems = server.sendmail(frim_addr, to_addr_list,
message)

server.quit()
```

When mail is sent, the output should be something of this sort:

Sample mail from sender:

```
sendemail(from_addr = "python@RC.net",
```

to_addr_list = ["RC@gmail.com"]

cc_addr_list = ["RC@xx.co.uk"]

subject= "Hello",

message= "Hello from a python function",

login= "pythonuser1"

password= "XXXXXX")

Sample mail received:

sendemail(from_addr = python@RC.net

to_addr_list = [RC@gmail.com]

cc_addr_list = [RC@xx.co.uk]

subject= "Hello",

message= "Hello from a python function",

login= "pythonuser1"

password= "XXXXXX"

• Password Generator with Python

Python strings alongside totally random modules can be used to generate passwords. The string module is comprised of sever useful constants and classes which would prove useful in this example. Some of them are:

1. string.ascii_letters: A combination of both uppercase and lowercase letters of the ASCII.

2. string.digits: The string numbers ranging from 0 to 9.

3. string.punctuation: A string of ASCII characters that are known to be punctuation characters in the C domain.

4. print string.ascii_letters

5. print string.digits

6. print string.punctuation

The output of the print is as follows:

abcdefghijklmnopqrstuvwxyzABCDEFGHIJKLMNOPQRST
UVWXYZ

0123456789

!"#$%&'()*+,-./:;<=>?@[]^_`{|}~

Password Generator Script:

To put the password generator together, we use the script written below:

import string

from random import *

characters = string.ascii_letters + string.punctuation + string.digits

password = '''.join(choice(characters) for x in range(randint(8, 16)))

print password

• **Search Tweets with Python**

In this example, we would be creating a script that would search for tweets using the Twitter API. We would be using JSON for this example, so it is vital for us to import the module. The screen name in Twitter has a similar screen name to the user for whom results would be returned for. When you enter the Twitter search URL, the result would be outputted in json format. The number of tweets can be obtained using the length function.

By the end of the script, the tweet would be parsed from the result and printed onto the screen.

```
#Importing the modules

import urllib2

import json

screen_name = 'wordpress'

url = 'http://api.twitter.com/1/statuses/user_timeline.json?scre
en_name=' + screen_name

data = json.load(urllib2.urlopen(url))

print len(data),

'tweets' for tweet in data:

print tweet["text"]
```

To promote interaction with the user, you can ask what tweet to search for from the user:

```
Screen = raw_input('Which tweet do you want to search? ')
```

CHAPTER 10: LEARN IT FASTER, REMEMBER IT LONGER

Learning is fun but being unable to recall what you learned when needed can be pretty frustrating. We have all had such moments in our lives when we desperately wanted to remember something but couldn't. It's almost like your brain experienced a total wipeout, even though that wasn't necessarily the case. So, what happened? Did you not learn it right, or are you unable to remember things? It could be either of these, or it could be on account of entirely different factors. We learn to remember and apply, but when all we do is forget, little to no progress is being made in the learning process. It is for this reason this section was created in this book. Python is easy to learn, fun even, but being unable to recall how to apply the knowledge you have garnered makes you no different from the average non-programmer.

So, without further ado, let's take a look at how you can remember the principles of Python long enough to be able to apply it usefully.

• Why are you learning Python?

Although this concept was discussed earlier in how to learn python section, it also applies to remembering what you have learned. The majority of the time, we learn things for other reasons but ourselves. If we can be honest with ourselves, many different decisions we have made in life are tied to a person or a cause outside of us. Why did you want to study medicine? Because your parents wanted you to. Why did you pick the college you attended? Because all your friends went there. Although this in no way implies that all your choices have been wrong, it begs the question; when was the last time you did something because you wanted to? For once, let your learning be a deliberate process. Let it be something you chose to do because you wanted it for a cause you love; not because you were influenced into it.

People tend to learn better and remember for longer when the choice to learn something is theirs. Because learning is a conscious process and being mindful of the things that influence you keeps you going. So, if you want to be a better learner of Python and not just any other learner, but one who remembers it enough to apply it, you have to know why you are learning Python. Also, the motive behind your reason is of high import to the learning process. Python is a powerful tool in the hand of whoever wields it, so, what is your driving force. Do you want to learn Python to satisfy a cause, or are you just learning it because it is what is required of you?

If your reason is the first option, you stand better chances of learning and remembering, the latter, on the other hand, less so.

- **Take it slow:**

Of course, there is such a thing as quick learning, and people can remember for long with it, but what if I told you learning doesn't have to happen at breakneck speed? Take a break and cut down on your pace. Don't feel under pressure to learn the basics of Python quickly. You aren't Barry Allen, and that's fine. Take your time to go through this book, learning the basics of Python one step at a time. If one chapter takes you a week to learn, flow with it. You are under no pressure to understand how Python works in record time. Van Rossum did not create Python in a day, so why would you feel under any form of pressure to learn it any faster? This doesn't mean that you should elongate the learning process longer than is typical, though. The point here is to learn at a pace that lets you learn, understand, and remember. And chugging yourself full of new knowledge is no way to do that. As you go through the chapters of this book, ensure that your goal is to learn, not to finish the book. Both are different things. It is one thing to read the book and learn from it, and another to finish the book like any other book out there. Apply mindfulness as you read, have the desire to learn from it, and if at any time you feel saturated, cut back, and relax. Relaxation is a crucial part of the learning process. It is why schools have breaks in their curriculums. If you feel overwhelmed, close the book, and breathe. You won't learn any better or remember more by pushing your limits, so you might as well avoid punishing yourself.

• Make a schedule for learning:

Do you know why schools break their curriculums across several weeks, and each week breaks into days which in turn break into school hours? It is because it facilitates learning. The school knows that if everything were to be compiled and delivered at once, it would only be overwhelming for the learners. Take this into perspective when reading this book. Make a schedule for how you want to learn the basics of Python. You can craft out some hours of the day to invest in learning with this book. It could be from an hour each day to as more as you can handle. Or you can schedule your learning according to chapters, say, one chapter a day. In making a schedule, though, ensure that you create one which suits you. Don't make a rigid schedule. Employ flexibility in your plan so you can be able to learn, take breaks, and still have time for other things. You must take breaks when learning to allow yourself time to rest and reinforce what you have learned. Also, schedule some time for reading and practicing. Alternate between theoretical learning and practical learning; it will help establish the knowledge you have gathered. So, before you get into studying this book, find a way to fit a learning period into your schedule that won't affect other areas of your life. Finding your balance is key to learning and remembering for longer.

• **Practice:**

The concept of practicing cannot be overly stressed in the learning process. You must often practice as you read this book. Not only would it help you learn more, but you would also remember better. If you must learn Python, you must be willing to take the time out to practice and become good at it. By practicing, you will learn the meaning of codes, their uses, and how they are applied in writing scripts. In your schedule, create a time you dedicate solely to practicing. It could be during the weekends. Say, for instance, if you study three days a week, you can take the time out of the weekends to practice what you have read. Also, seeing as python programming is a practical-demanding field, it is necessary that you have as much theoretical experience as you do practically. Learning the theoretical part of Python alone will not suffice to ground you in the knowledge of it. So, take heed that you do not build your knowledge of Python on theory alone.

• Test Yourself:

Just as schools have a period in which they test learners on what they have learned, you should also craft out time to test yourself. You need to know your learning prowess over time as you study this book. Knowing it will help you know whether or not you are making any significant progress. So, make out time to test your skills both theoretically and practically. Will you be able to give a concise account of what you have learned by heart? Can you expressly create an error-free script that can be executed? Test yourself on many levels, oral or written, by having someone drill you on questions related to python programming. Feel free to set your drills as often as you want, but don't let it interfere with your schedule. In your plans, make out a specific time specially dedicated to testing your knowledge. Judge yourself according to your results from the tests, so you can know areas you need to strengthen or relearn.

- **Broaden your horizons:**

Don't stay limited to this book alone. Python is an evolving language and being stuck on the content of this book alone doesn't bode well for you as a learner. Broaden your horizons in terms of learning. After studying this handbook, go ahead and check other texts for more knowledge. Don't stop learning Python the moment you finish with this book. There is more to learn about Python, so don't limit yourself to this book alone. Groom your knowledge by contacting different sources for more materials. Speak to Python experts. Get mentored by a professional. Join a team of Python programmers. Just engage yourself in more learning. Knowledge thrives when engaged, so don't hesitate to indulge in anything which helps you know more. There are many ways Python can be applied, and in broadening your horizons, you find more ways to apply it. In turn, this helps you grow as a learner and programmer. In the end, evolve as a programmer. Employ new methods in solving issues and watch yourself grow.

CONCLUSION

My sincerest thanks for including this book in your collection.

I believe that on completion of this book, you will have understood the basics of Python programming, and be prepared to embark onto the next phase of understanding and working with Python.

www.ingramcontent.com/pod-product-compliance
Lightning Source LLC
Chambersburg PA
CBHW071118050326
40690CB00008B/1266